DEAD FAMOUS

ALEXANDER THE GREAT

AND HIS CLAIM TO FAME

by **Phil Robins**

Illustrated by Clive Goddard

Hippo

For Toby, Joseph, Jonathan and
(of course) Alexander

Scholastic Children's Books,
Euston House, 24 Eversholt Street,
London NW1 1DB, UK

A division of Scholastic Ltd
London ~ New York ~ Toronto ~ Sydney ~ Auckland
Mexico City ~ New Delhi ~ Hong Kong

Published in the UK by Scholastic UK Ltd, 2005

Text copyright © Phil Robins 2005
Illustrations copyright © Clive Goddard, 2005

ISBN 10: 0 439 96349 4
ISBN 13: 978 0439 96349 7

Printed in the UK by CPI Bookmarque, Croydon, CR0 4TD

6 8 10 9 7 5

The right of Phil Robins and Clive Goddard to be identified as the
author and illustrator respectively of this work has been asserted by them
in accordance with the Copyright, Designs and Patents Act, 1988.

Papers used by Scholastic Children's Books are made
from wood grown in sustainable forests

INTRODUCTION

You might have heard of Alexander the Great, but how much do you know about him? For a start, why was he so great? Just what *is* his claim to fame?

HE WAS A GREAT LEADER!

HE WAS A GREAT CONQUEROR!

HE WAS A GREAT... ER... GREEK BLOKE.

Over the centuries, thousands of books have been written about Alexander and sometimes his exploits have been exaggerated and turned into legendary adventures.

According to some stories, Alexander not only flew to heaven in a basket carried by eagles, but also went underwater in the world's first submarine!

Unfortunately Alexander wasn't quite *that* great, but although the facts are a bit more down to earth, they're still pretty amazing.

Alexander was King of Macedonia (in Greece), and his main claim to fame is that he led a huge army of Greek soldiers and marched them over burning deserts and freezing mountain ranges to the furthest reaches of the known world, conquering just about everything in his path. As a result he ruled over a vast empire of more than two million square miles that stretched all the way from the River Danube in Europe to what is now Pakistan. And he did all this before dying at the ripe old age of just 32!

Without a doubt, Alexander was a brilliant military leader and for some people that's enough for him to go down in history as genuinely 'great'. But others argue that Alexander doesn't deserve his nickname. (After all, nobody *asked* him to come and conquer them.) According to these people, Alexander was just a bully who terrorized people into doing what he wanted, and who drove his army for thousands of miles just so he could get his name in the history books.

There's no doubt about it: in many ways, Alexander *wasn't* very nice. For instance:

• he had a terrible temper and once killed one of his best friends in a drunken rage

• he had several of his men – including one of his top generals – murdered in cold blood

• he punished several 'enemy' cities by destroying them completely

• he ended up getting so bigheaded that he declared he wasn't simply a man, but actually a god!

On the other hand, he wasn't *all* bad. He was loyal to many of his friends (those he *didn't* kill), and treated many of his enemies kindly (er … those he didn't execute). And of course he lived at a time when it was more or less expected that kings would act ruthlessly now and then. It was just the way things were done in those days.

Still, this book isn't *all* murder and mayhem – it'll tell you a few other things about the great man as well: How did he get on at school? What was his favourite bedtime reading? How did he meet his favourite horse? The details are all here. Of course, there's also plenty about his astounding achievements on the battlefield and his extraordinary journey to the ends of the earth. And if it's the inside story you're after, you'll even get to see his Secret Diary *and* his letters to his mum!

BUT ONLY IF YOU PROMISE NOT TO TELL.

LITTLE ALEX

Baby Alex was born in July 356 BC, in Pella, the capital city of Macedonia – a small country in northern Greece where his father, Philip, was the king.

Philip was a ferocious, hard-drinking man with a reputation for toughness, but he was also a highly successful ruler, much admired by his countrymen for his skill as a warrior and a general. (Mind you, he *was* careless enough to lose one of his eyes in battle.)

Philip was married to several wives (which was allowed in those days), including Alex's beautiful mother, Olympias. A princess from a country called Epirus, just outside Macedonia, Olympias was an ambitious, determined lady, with quite a temper. She soon earned a reputation as someone you didn't mess with if you had any sense, and, to the Macedonians, she also seemed a strange, exotic woman. This was partly because she was a foreigner, and partly because she was dead keen on weird mystical ceremonies involving lots of frenzied dancing with her collection of pet snakes. King Philip wasn't really into that sort of thing, and his wife's peculiar hobbies soon put a strain on their marriage – especially after he woke up one morning to find a snake in his bed!

GET ME OUT OF HERE!

Despite their disagreements, Philip and Olympias both loved Alex to bits and wanted to see him grow up to be king one day. One of Philip's other wives had already given him a son – named Arrhidaeus – but unfortunately he suffered from a mental disability. That meant Alex was the favourite to succeed Philip, even though he was the younger of the two brothers, and Olympias was determined to keep it that way. (Alex also had several sisters, but they stood no chance of inheriting the throne because women weren't considered suitable rulers in Ancient Greece.)

> GREAT STORIES: ARRHIDAEUS
> Some people believe that the reason Alex's half-brother was disabled was because Olympias poisoned him when he was a baby. There's no hard evidence for this, but it's certainly possible. Olympias, as we'll see, was a ruthless woman who would do almost anything to ensure that *her* boy – and no one else's – would one day get to be king.

SuperAlex

Unfortunately, we don't know much about Alex's early years, but no doubt he spent a lot of time playing in the corridors and gardens of the palace at Pella. Here he would have first learned to wrestle and fight, as well as ride horses and hunt for wild animals. (Mind you, one thing he wasn't very good at was swimming, something he would *never* get the hang of.) Here too he would have first learned to honour the gods who were worshipped throughout Greece.

GREAT TIMES: GREEK GODS

The Greeks didn't just have one god, they had lots of different ones, each with their own temples. The 12 most important were believed to live on Olympus, the highest mountain in Greece. They included…

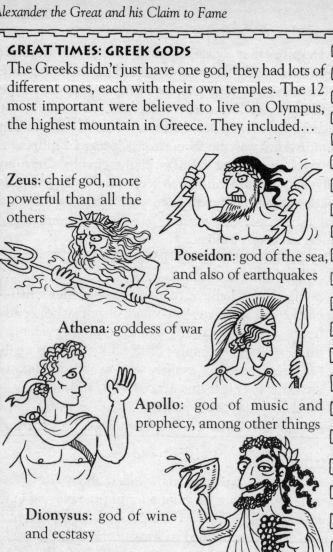

Zeus: chief god, more powerful than all the others

Poseidon: god of the sea, and also of earthquakes

Athena: goddess of war

Apollo: god of music and prophecy, among other things

Dionysus: god of wine and ecstasy

Everybody had their favourite gods, but they honoured and respected all of them. The most obvious way to do this was to make a sacrifice by killing an animal and offering the gods some of the fat and bones.

12

As he was growing up, Alex would have heard all about the gods, especially Zeus and Dionysus, two of his mum's favourites. (It was Dionysus she was worshipping when she danced with her snakes. And when she was feeling especially cross with her husband, she sometimes told Alex that Zeus was his real father, not Philip!)

Alex would also have heard plenty about the *human* heroes of Greek myth and legend. If he'd written a diary, perhaps it would have looked something like this…

Alexander's Secret Diary
Aged 7 and 3/4

Mum told me a great story last night, before she kissed me goodnight. It was all about a superhero called ~~Hetaces~~ Heracles, who lived long, long ago.

Heracles travelled about all over the place and was brilliant at killing monsters and things – sometimes with his bare hands.

The best bit was when he killed the Hydra,

a monster with loads of heads. Mummy says one day I'll be big and strong just like Heracles, and people will be telling stories about me!

GRR! GRR! GRR!

GREAT TIMES: HERACLES

To the Greeks, Heracles was a sort of comic-book superhero, and they had loads of stories about his adventures. He was especially famous for being fearless and strong, and for overcoming impossible difficulties. According to legend, Heracles didn't die, but actually turned into a god instead. He was especially popular in Macedonia because he was supposed to be an ancestor of the Macedonian royal family.

Superpower

While Alex was still listening to bedtime stories, his father Philip was busy winning a few real battles. He was in the process of turning Macedonia from a fairly unimportant country on the fringes of Greece into the most powerful state in the ancient world.

In those days, Greece wasn't a single country like it is today, but a collection of small, separate states, many of which were known as 'city-states'.

GREAT TIMES: CITY-STATES

City-states were tiny countries with just one city, each with its own government and army. The most famous of them was probably Athens, but Sparta and Thebes followed close behind. They were always competing against each other – and sometimes actually fighting one another – in the hope of proving themselves top dogs in Greece.

For the past few hundred years, the city-states had looked down rather snobbishly on Macedonia (which wasn't actually a city-state itself, but a bigger country with a capital city at Pella). This was partly because Macedonia wasn't rich or powerful, and partly because it hadn't so far made any great contributions to Greek civilization, whereas the city-states – particularly Athens – had produced world-famous writers, philosophers and sportsmen by the bucketload.

Another reason for the snobbery was that Macedonia wasn't a 'democracy'. Democracy means 'rule by the people' and it was an Athenian invention that they were really proud of. Instead of having a single king bossing everyone about and always getting his way, the Athenians used a system of voting to make decisions a bit fairer. (Mind you, neither women nor slaves got a vote, so it wasn't *that* fair.) Before long the system had caught on among many of the other city-states, but Macedonia still had an old-fashioned king in charge, and many Greeks – especially in Athens – thought this was *very* backward.

On top of all that, the Macedonians spoke with a gruff northern accent that was difficult for other Greeks to understand, and they'd also picked up a reputation for yobbish behaviour and drinking far too much. As a result, many Greeks from further south considered the Macedonians to be uncivilized oiks who hardly deserved to be thought of as 'Greek' at all.

But all this began to change under the rule of King Philip, who cleverly played on the rivalry between the Greek city-states to make Macedonia much more powerful and important. Philip didn't care two hoots about democracy, and was determined to rule Macedonia – and eventually the rest of Greece as well – with a rod of iron. He soon beefed up the Macedonian army, turning it into one of the most formidable fighting forces in the ancient world. And thanks to his skill as a politician and his ruthless use of his power as king, Macedonia eventually emerged as the new 'superpower' in Greece.

Alex wins his spurs

As the years passed, it wasn't just Macedonia that was winning respect. One story in particular tells how the 12-year-old Alex – even though he was small for his age – was already beginning to impress people with his courage.

1 One day Philip took Alex along with him to a horse fair.

2 Philip liked the look of one horse, but when he came near it reared up at him.

3 However, Alex had taken a shine to the horse…

4 Alex turned the horse towards the sun, so it couldn't see its shadow any more, and somehow managed to calm it down.

5 Then he threw his cloak on the horse's back, vaulted up, and the two of them tore off across the plain…

6 After a few minutes, Alex returned, riding the horse with expert control.

WELL, SON, YOU'D BETTER FIND YOURSELF A BIGGER KINGDOM THAN THIS ONE. MACEDONIA IS GOING TO BE **MUCH** TOO SMALL FOR YOU!

Philip was so pleased with his son that he gave him the horse as a present – and Alex named his new friend Bucephalas (which means 'ox's head') because he was branded with a horse-dealer's mark in the shape of an ox. The pair soon became inseparable and it would be Bucephalas who would later carry Alex on all his adventures and into every one of his important battles.

SCHOOL DAYS

King Philip was often away from Pella – either leading his armies into battle against neighbouring states or on diplomatic missions far from home, and the young Alex tended to see a lot more of his mother than his father. Olympias took every opportunity to make a fuss of her son and spoil him rotten, but she also appointed home-tutors for the young boy to help him with his education. Alex's first tutor was a tough little man called Leonidas, a real stickler for the rules. He saw it as his job to toughen Alex up, and was a great one for brisk early-morning runs and a strict diet…

GREAT!

Leonidas also spent much of his time hunting through Alex's things, in case his mother had slipped him any forbidden treats!

GREAT STORIES: A SPICY TALE

According to one story, Alex was one day burning some sweet-smelling incense in a temple and Leonidas ticked him off for using too much. He told him he had no right to waste it, as he hadn't yet conquered Asia, the region where incense and other exotic spices came from.

The story goes that years later, when Alex *had* conquered Asia, he remembered this and sent Leonidas a present of *18 tons* of precious frankincense and myrrh. He told him there was no longer any need to be stingy to the gods!

In spite of Leonidas' strictness, young Alex also found time for pursuing his favourite hobbies, including hunting and music-making. Like his hero Heracles, Alex was a keen hunter, and he was always coming home dragging a dead animal or two behind him. Alex also liked to play the lyre (an instrument a bit like a small harp) but, like swimming, music was never one of his strong points. Even after Olympias had put him down for lyre lessons he showed little sign of improvement.

21

According to one story, Alex once asked his music teacher if it really *mattered* whether he played one particular note rather than another. The teacher told him that for future kings it did not matter, but for musicians it did – a polite hint that Alex was no musician!

Alex in the classroom

Before long, King Philip decided to send Alex away to school in the countryside, along with some other children from rich Macedonian families. This wasn't just so that his lyre-playing was well out of earshot – it was also to get Alex further away from his mum, who continued to spoil him. And, of course, Philip also wanted to give his son the best education that money could buy.

For a teacher, Philip brought in a famous old philosopher from Athens called Aristotle, a scarily clever man. Among the lessons on Aristotle's school timetable were these: Medicine, Natural History (Biology), Geography, Politics, Greek Literature, Physics, Astronomy, Philosophy and Rhetoric (how to make fantastic speeches and win arguments by using words cleverly). And that was just *before* breaktime!

Being taught by a clever-dick like Aristotle can't have been easy, and especially not for Alex, who was an active sort, rather than a deep thinker.

Alexander's Secret Diary
Summer 343 BC (Aged 13)

Lessons are mostly boring, boring, boring, but sometimes we have a laugh. Me and Hephaistion - he's my best friend - have worked out a great game where we swap seats every time Aristotle's back is turned. You should see the look on his face while he's trying to work out what's going on!

I suppose the old man's all right really, even if he does keep confiscating my lyre. 'Ever strive to be the best', that's what he's always telling us. And the best is exactly what I'm going to be. Not the best at <u>school</u>, though. (That's just for wimps and swots.) I want to be the best <u>king</u> of all time.

Best

In fact, Alex did learn a lot from Aristotle's lessons, and in the end the old teacher had quite an influence on him. For a start, he made him read a book which might have looked a bit boring at first, but soon became Alex's number-one favourite story of all time.

GREAT TIMES: HOMER'S ILIAD

This book, believed to have been composed by a blind poet hundreds of years before Alexander was born, was the most well-known story in the Greek world. It was about a long and bitter war between the Greeks and the Trojans – the people who lived in the city of Troy in Asia Minor (modern Turkey).

The story began when the Trojan prince Paris stole the beautiful Helen from her Greek husband Menelaus, King of Sparta.

In revenge, a bunch of Greek kings got together and assembled a huge army that sailed to Troy and lay siege to it for several years. (A siege is when an army surrounds a city and cuts off its supplies.)

Eventually the Greeks entered Troy, destroyed the city and returned Helen to her husband.

OH, TA.

In fact, most of the *Iliad* is actually set on the 'windy plains' of Troy, during the actual siege, so there are lots of battle-scenes and plenty of blood and guts.

THE MAIN GREEK FIGHTER IS CALLED ACHILLES.

ACHILLES HAD A BAD TEMPER, AND AT THE BEGINNING HE SULKS IN HIS TENT.

BUT IN THE END HE LEADS THE GREEKS TO VICTORY.

HELPED BY HIS BEST FRIEND PATROCULUS, OF COURSE!

There's no doubt that if Alexander had been cast away on a desert island, the *Iliad* is the book he would have liked to have with him, and when he was on his campaigns in Asia he always slept with a copy of it under his pillow!

In fact, Alex soon began to see himself as a second Achilles – another hero who was destined to win glory for the Greeks in war. (He might have been encouraged in this by another one of his tutors, a man named Lysimachus, who actually called him Achilles instead of Alexander. The reason for this was that Olympias, Alex's mum, was supposed to be *descended* from Achilles, which meant Alex was as well. So that was *two* superheroes he was related to!)

Achilles' Secret Diary (No, not really. It's just me!!)

While I'm stuck here at school, Dad's winning one great victory after another. I hope he leaves a few battles for <u>me</u> to win! Hephaistion says I shouldn't complain. Dad's making Macedonia rich and powerful so that I can take over one day. But I don't just want power, I want adventures. I want to be a <u>superhero</u>, not a boring old king with nothing to do.

Of course, Alex would one day find plenty to do, and it was probably in Aristotle's Geography lessons that he first learnt where to look for his best chance to have some adventures like Achilles:

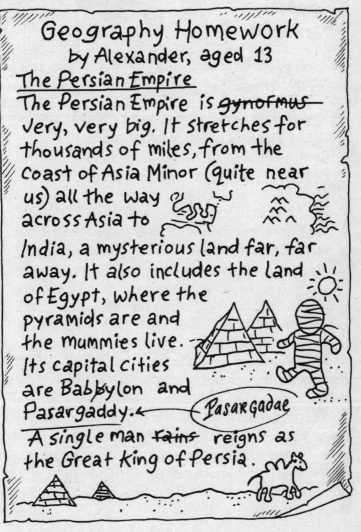

Geography Homework
by Alexander, aged 13
The Persian Empire

The Persian Empire is ~~gynofmus~~ very, very big. It stretches for thousands of miles, from the coast of Asia Minor (quite near us) all the way across Asia to India, a mysterious land far, far away. It also includes the land of Egypt, where the pyramids are and the mummies live. Its capital cities are Babbylon and Pasargaddy. — Pasargadae

A single man ~~rains~~ reigns as the Great King of Persia.

GREAT TIMES: GREEKS V BARBARIANS

To the Greeks, all non-Greeks were known as 'barbarians'. At first, this just meant something like 'people who don't speak Greek' (which doesn't sound half so rude). However, many Greeks thought that Greek was the only proper language and that only by speaking Greek – and for that matter, *being* Greek – could anyone hope to achieve *anything* worthwhile. In fact they came to believe they were the absolute bees' knees in every department, and soon decided that barbarians weren't just *different*, but completely inferior.

Persian civilization was actually just as old as that of the Greeks, and just as interesting and impressive, but the Greeks were terrible snobs. And though you might think a top brain like Aristotle would know better, he was actually one of the worst snobs of all and constantly drilled it into Alexander that the Persians were a race of no-hopers who deserved to be conquered and licked into shape by the mighty Greeks.

GREAT TIMES: GREEKS V PERSIANS

For the Greeks, everything good that could be said about them found its opposite in the Persians. So while the Greeks were supposedly tough, strong and self-controlled, the Persians were weak-willed and soft. The Greeks were calm and logical, but the Persians were hot-headed. The Greeks didn't eat and drink too much – 'all things in moderation' was one of Aristotle's favourite sayings – whereas the Persians got carried away and did things to excess.

Of course, one reason the Greeks were so down on the Persians was because they felt threatened by them. After all, the Persian Empire wasn't far away from Greece, and it had an enormous army. In fact, Greece had once been invaded by the Persians, a humiliation that they'd never forgotten, and something else that Alex would have learned about at school...

History Homework
by Alexander, aged 15

Boing

The Persian Wars
In 490, about 150 years ago, the Persian king Darius I invaded Greece but he was beaten at the battle of Marathon. Ten years later his son Xerxes attacked again and this time he

even managed to get inside the city of Athens and set fire to it. But then the Persian fleet was smashed to smithereens at the battle of Salamis, and then we finally bashed up the Persian army at Plataea, bringing the Persian Wars to an end.

We Greeks haven't got our own back properly yet, but we will one day, especially when I'm in charge! One day we'll conquer the whole Persian Empire!

✓ VERY GOOD, BUT PLEASE TRY TO USE MORE APPROPRIATE LANGUAGE.

Alexander must have spent a lot of time gazing out of his classroom window, daydreaming about such adventures (especially when Aristotle was droning on about equilateral triangles or something). However, it was going to be some time before Alex got a chance to do any conquering. And in the meantime, he wasn't even sure he'd ever even get the chance to take over from his dad as King of Macedonia…

October 342 BC

Dear Alex,

I hope you're being a good boy and getting on with your studies.

Your father came home yesterday, but he's hardly said a word to me and spent all his time with those other sorry excuses for wives. I'm not jealous, of course – but I don't want him having another son who'll be a rival to you, dear. I told him as much, but he just said: 'It will do no harm for the boy to have some competition.' Well, we'll see about that. Stupid man!

In the meantime, you'd better pay attention to everything that nice Mr Aristotle says. You never know when it might come in handy.

Lots of love and kisses,

Mummy xxx

PS Strive to be the best, sweetie, and one day you'll have the world at your feet.

PPS You're not still trying to play that lyre, are you?

HAPPY FAMILIES

By the time he was 16, Alex had finished school and his father decided he was ready for more responsibility. So when Philip next went away to fight in nearby Thrace he left his son to look after Macedonia for him. An old family friend called Antipater was also appointed to advise the young man, but for the first time in his life Alexander found himself in charge, and he loved every minute of it:

December 340 BC

Dear Dad,
Don't worry. All's well here at home. We had a bit of bother with a rebellious northern tribe last week, but I soon sorted it. I even captured a rebel city and decided to rename it after me. Yes, it's now called 'Alexandropolis'. (Nice ring to it, eh?) How's it going with those upstart

Thracians? If you want me to come and help you sort them out, just let me know.

Respectfully,
Alexander

January 339 BC

Dear Son,

It sounds like you're doing a fine job. However, I must ask you not to name any more cities after yourself. That is for _me_ to do. (You'll have plenty of time for that sort of thing when _you're_ king.)

And don't spend _too_ much time chasing rebels. At your age you should be enjoying yourself.

With love, Dad

PS Watch out for _your_ mother's blasted snakes. I found one in my luggage the other day!

Alex makes his mark

As Macedonian power increased, a showdown between Philip and the still-powerful city-states of Athens and Thebes was inevitable. It finally came in the year 338 BC, at the great battle of Chaeronea. Here, the Macedonians were finally able to prove that thanks to Philip's reforms, they had the most effective army in all of Greece. This is what it looked like:

INFANTRY UNITS, EACH KNOWN AS A 'PHALANX'

5-METRE PIKES KNOWN AS 'SARISSAS'

HEDGEHOG FORMATION OF OVERLAPPING SARISSAS

CAVALRY DIVISIONS IN TIGHT 'WEDGE' FORMATION - DIFFICULT TO BREAK DOWN

At Chaeronea, Philip decided that Alex, who was now 18, should fight in the battle as a cavalry captain. No doubt the young man was delighted with the starring role he played in the day's events.

August 338 BC

Dear Mum,

You'll be ever so proud of me. Dad put me in probably the most important position in the whole army, in charge of hundreds of men fighting on horseback. Bucephalas was magnificent and, thanks to us, we soon showed those upstart Greeks who's boss.

Only one thing spoiled my day: after the battle we were celebrating with a jar of wine, and while I was entertaining everyone with a few of my best lyre-tunes Dad got completely drunk. He finished up tottering around the battlefield, among the corpses, shouting at the top of his voice. It was <u>So</u> embarrassing!

Honestly, Mum, you'll have to have a word with him. What kind of behaviour is that from the king of Macedonia?

With love,
Alex xxx

To make amends for his unseemly behaviour – which had made him look more like a hooligan than a world statesman – Philip decided to make a grand public gesture. So he released 2,000 Athenian prisoners and announced that he would send home to Athens the ashes of the thousand Athenian soldiers who had died at Chaeronea. And it was Alexander who was given the job of carrying out this important mission…

A common enemy

Philip next decided to organize a big peace conference where he forced the city-states to join something called the 'Corinthian League'. This had nothing to do with football – it was just an official agreement to be friends, drawn up at a place called Corinth.

In theory the League was a group of allies with no single state in charge, but in practice everyone knew that Macedonia called the shots. And although the city-states *said* they wanted peace, Philip knew that they hated Macedonia and were already plotting against him in secret. What he needed was a way to distract them from their rebellious ways and unite them more solidly under his leadership. But how could he do that?

As it happened, he'd recently received a piece of friendly advice from a wise old Athenian politician named Isocrates.

Autumn 346 BC

Dear Philip,
Why don't you ask the other Greek states to join you in a crusade against the PERSIANS? After all, it would be better to fight the Great King for his Asian Empire than squabble amongst ourselves, don't you think? And of course, if you conquered Persia you'd be more powerful than ever. In fact, I reckon you'd be more or less like a God!
Your friend,
Isocrates of Athens

Isocrates' suggestion certainly made sense. After all…
• Most Greeks agreed that the Persians were foreigners and barbarians, and Philip could see that it would be easy to unite everybody against them.
• The Great King of Persia was well known for his fabulous wealth, and the idea of getting their hands on it appealed to just about *everyone* in Greece.
• The humiliation of the 'Persian Wars' was still a sore point and many Greeks felt they had a score to settle. Philip could therefore claim to be planning a general Greek war of revenge against the Persians, even though his real motive was to extend *Macedonian* power and put a stop to Greek rebellions against *him*.

• Many cities of Asia Minor were actually Greek cities, founded by Greek settlers centuries earlier but now living under Persian rule. Their citizens had mostly grown used to the Persians and few were actually crying out to be set free, but Philip could pretend he was doing everybody a favour by kicking the Persians out.

All in all, it was the perfect solution, and Philip soon made his plans known throughout Greece.

Two weddings and a funeral

Unfortunately, just as Philip was making peace with the city-states of Greece, his own family was having a dreadful row – one that may have ended up costing him his life. It all started when he finally fell out with Olympias.

Philip soon found a replacement he liked the look of – a posh Macedonian girl called Eurydice (*yoo-riddy-see*), the niece of one of his top generals – and within weeks he'd announced that they were going to get married.

Alexander's Secret Diary
September 338 BC

What a disaster. Dad's totally in love with this new girl – and Mum's furious. She reckons she's been given the push because she's a foreigner, whereas Eurydice is from an old Macedonian family.

And apparently people are saying that if he and this new girl have a son, he'll be the real heir to the throne, not me, because he'll be of pure Macedonian blood.

But that's not fair! Surely *I'M* destined to be the next king, aren't I? Everybody knows that. (In fact, Hephaistion says he's heard some people say that they wish Dad was their general, and *I* was their *king*.)

In true Macedonian style, there was plenty to eat and drink at the royal wedding, but the atmosphere was still a bit strained…

The worst moment was when Attalus, Eurydice's uncle, proposed a toast to the new couple and their future baby:

Alexander knew he'd gone too far, and that night he and his mother fled from Philip's court at Pella and left the country altogether. Alexander left his mum with relatives in Epirus, while he went into hiding in Illyria, to the north of Macedonia. For the next few months, he was in disgrace, and exiled from his father's court.

October 338 BC

Dear Hephaistion
Oh great! Me and my big mouth!
I'm never going to be king now, am I?
What a disaster. And now I'm stuck
in this gods-forsaken place, with
nothing to do but practise on my lyre,
just when things are getting interesting.
Dad's about to send an advance party
to Asia to prepare a landing spot for
the rest of the army. It won't be long
before the real invasion begins. And
I'm going to miss it!

Well, keep me posted... I want
to hear all the gossip.
Alex

Back in Macedonia, Eurydice soon became pregnant, but when the baby was born it turned out to be a girl, which from Philip's point of view was no use at all, since girls couldn't succeed to the Macedonian throne. Philip now decided that perhaps Alexander was his best bet for a successor after all, and tried to repair his relationship with his son. (Apart from anything else, he was uneasy

41

about setting off for Asia with Alexander still fuming in Illyria, where he might stir up a rebellion against him.)

Spring 337 BC

Dear Son,

All this arguing is silly. How can I talk about harmony between Greeks if my own family is at each other's throats?

So why don't you come home, eh? I'm going to need your help against the Persians. And needless to say, you <u>are</u> my chosen successor, there's no need to worry about that.

Dad

PS Perhaps it'd be best if you left your mother where she is.

So Alex moved back to Pella and helped his dad, while his mum remained in exile.

However, Philip soon began to worry that Olympias might persuade her brother, the King of Epirus, to make trouble against him, even though he was meant to be an ally. With the invasion due any time soon, the last thing he wanted was a war with one of his neighbours. So he soon proposed that the two states cement their friendship with a marriage between the King of Epirus and Philip's own daughter Cleopatra (one of Alex's sisters).

Once this was agreed, Philip was determined to put on a good show to impress everyone with his wealth and importance. Invitations were sent out to ambassadors and VIPs from all over Greece, while the ancient city of Aegae was decked out in all sorts of finery in preparation for a huge marriage-feast complete with public games, music festivals (where Alex would have a chance to show off his lyre-playing) and sacrifices to the gods.

Spring 336 BC

Dear Mum,
As it's such a special occasion, Dad's asked me to invite you to the wedding. (Though he says can you please leave the snakes behind.) You will come, won't you? I've got lots I want to talk to you about. For a start, Eurydice's just given birth to a baby boy, and Dad's absolutely over the moon - which is a bit worrying. Worse still, he's decided to call him Caranus. It didn't mean anything to me until Hephaistion pointed out that it was the name of the very first Macedonian king! So it sounds like Dad might have big plans for him, after all.
    Honestly, I can't believe I'm in competition with a baby!
    Look forward to seeing you soon.
Much love, Alex x x x

Olympias certainly did come to the wedding, along with hundreds of guests from all over Greece. It was quite an occasion, with plenty of feasting and drinking, and at first everybody seemed to have a good time. However, on the morning of the second day of celebrations, tragedy struck:

The Macedonian Mail

NOW AVAILABLE THROUGHOUT GREECE - SPECIAL EDITION - JUNE 336 BC

MURDER MOST FOUL!

- King Stabbed To Death At Royal Wedding Feast
- One Man Arrested

All of Greece is in shock today following the brutal assassination of King Philip of Macedonia. The King was attacked early this morning by one of his own bodyguards while celebrating the marriage of his daughter. Doctors rushed to the scene but the King suffered multiple stab wounds and is believed to have died almost instantly.

The King was taking part in a special procession when the attack occurred. At its head, officials carried statues of the 12 gods of Olympus, while a thirteenth — in the likeness of King Philip himself — followed closely behind. (A palace official has denied rumours that the King was claiming to be a god.)

It was just after Philip joined the procession, clad in a white ceremonial cloak, that the assassin struck.

A man was apprehended after fleeing the scene and executed on the spot.

The country is now in uproar, though Prince Alexander — who spent the night in consultation with close friends and advisers — is favourite to take over.

Moments after the attack

WIN A HOLIDAY FOR TWO IN ATHENS! INSIDE, PAGE 33.

GREAT STORIES: THE MURDER OF KING PHILIP
No one knows for sure who was behind the murder. The bodyguard who killed him was called Pausanias, and it was said he'd had a row with Philip which led to the attack. However, it's certainly possible that Pausanias was paid by someone else to commit the crime. Here are some of the suspects:

Suspect A: The Great
King of Persia

Motive: to kill
Philip before he had
a chance to launch
his invasion.

Suspect B: Alexander

Motive: to become
king before being
bypassed in favour
of Caranus.

Suspect C: Olympias

Motive: to make sure
her son becomes king
while Caranus is
still a baby and to
get revenge for
being dumped.

No one knows for sure, but most people think Olympias
was probably behind the murder. She was a thoroughly
ruthless woman, prepared to do almost anything to see
her son succeed.

ALEX TAKES CHARGE

Alexander, now aged 20, might have seemed the obvious person to take over from Philip, especially as Caranus was still a baby, but not everyone saw it that way. Some people thought that Philip's nephew Amyntas should be king, while others wanted a grown-up 'guardian' to look after the throne until Caranus was old enough to take over. But as well as loyal friends like Hephaistion, Alexander had the support of two crucial people: Philip's trusted adviser Antipater, and his top general Parmenio. With their help he acted speedily to make sure the throne was his.

Firstly, Antipater presented Alexander before the Macedonian army, who gave him their support in the traditional way.

THE KING IS DEAD. LONG LIVE THE KING

Then, Alex made a big show of punishing anyone connected with Pausanias, the man who was publicly blamed for his father's murder. First his three sons were executed, even though they had nothing to do with it, and then his *horses* were put to death!

WELL, YOU CAN'T BE TOO CAREFUL, CAN YOU?

In fact, Alexander spent most of the first year of his reign giving orders for the execution of his enemies, or anyone he thought might be a threat to him. (Among them was Attalus, the man who'd upset Alex at his father's wedding by making it clear that he didn't want Alex to be king.) Alex would soon become world famous for his bravery and his brilliant tactics, but sheer ruthlessness was also a reason for his success. He was determined to take over where his father had left off – especially when it came to launching the Asian invasion – and he wasn't going to let anyone stand in his way.

Alex gets busy

Alex had his work cut out, though, because Philip's death was followed by a wave of rebellions against Macedonia in Greece and among her northern neighbours. No one yet realized that Alexander was going to be even tougher than his father. Instead, many thought they saw a chance to break free of the Macedonian rule they had had to put up with under Philip.

Alexander's Secret Diary
October 336 BC

A few weeks ago, when Dad was still alive, the Athenians were bending over backwards to please him. But as soon as they heard he was dead they announced a day of public celebrations!

Hephaistion says they've even asked the Great King of Persia for money to help them in a rebellion against me! But if they think they're going to have an easy time of it now that I'm in charge, they've got another think coming.

Alex soon got busy, marching his Macedonian army up and down Greece stamping out rebellions left, right and centre. In the process, he showed everyone just how brilliant he was at getting out of a tight spot using clever tactics. Here's how he achieved five of his early successes in northern Greece…

1 Thessaly. Alexander approaches the Thessalian leaders in a well-defended mountain pass. The Thessalians think they are in a strong position and tell him they might consider supporting him if he asks nicely.

Alex gets his engineers to cut a stairway up the steep sides of the mountain pass. The Thessalians are soon cornered and forced to accept his conditions.

2 Thrace. The Thracians line up wagons at the head of a steep pass, threatening to push them down and crush Alexander and his men. Alexander orders his men to lie down under their shields, and the wagons bounce over them harmlessly. Then they storm the pass and defeat the Thracians.

3 Triballia. The Triballians occupy a wooded glen near a river, a good defensive position.

Alexander hides his main army and sends a tiny force of archers and slingers to lure the Triballians from their position. Then the main army moves in and cuts them to pieces.

4 Getae nomads. The nomads have massed in their thousands, waiting for Alexander on the far side of the River Danube.

Alexander orders his men to build dug-out canoes from tree-trunks and to make rafts with tent-covers stuffed with hay. He ferries 6,000 men and 1,500 horses across the Danube by night and terrifies the nomads into running away.

5 Illyria. Illyrian tribesmen have occupied hills surrounding Alexander and his army, trapping them.

Alexander orders his army to form up in close ranks and carry out close-order drill with their sarissas. With absolute discipline, and in total silence, the men put up their sarissas into a vertical salute and then move them down to battle position.

51

The Illyrians are fascinated by this display, and – as if hypnotized – gradually edge closer. At Alexander's pre-arranged signal his cavalry let out the terrifying Macedonian war cry and charge headlong.

The Illyrians drop their weapons and run.

Alex also marched his army to Corinth where he forced the Greek states to do three things:
1 Renew the League set up by his father.
2 Pledge their loyalty to *him* instead.
3 Agree to press on with Philip's plans for an attack on the Persian Empire.

GREAT STORIES: DIOGENES

While he was in Corinth, Alex had time for a bit of sightseeing, and one of the most famous sights the city had to offer was a famous philosopher known as Diogenes (*dye-oj-uh-nees*) the Cynic. He was quite a celebrity at the time and had earned his nickname (which means 'Diogenes the Dog') because he'd decided to renounce the world of men and live like an animal, which mainly meant lying in the sun doing nothing. He believed in living as simply as possible, without things like money and possessions and other complications. Basically, he was a sort of Ancient Greek hippy, who survived by begging, and when Alexander met him he was living by the side of the road in a large storage jar.

Here's what happened…

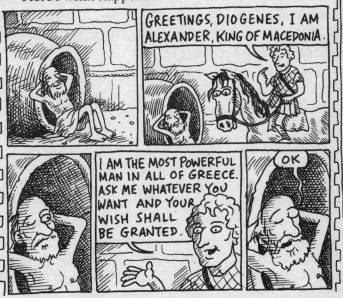

Luckily Alex was in a good mood and didn't get cross. In fact, he was so pleased with Diogenes' reply that he announced that if he could be anyone in the world except Alexander, he'd like to be him!

Invincible Alex

On the way back from Corinth, Alexander also found time to stop off at Delphi to consult the famous Delphic oracle.

GREAT TIMES: ORACLES

Oracles were special shrines where the Greeks went to ask the gods for their advice, often about future plans. (Visiting an oracle was a bit like reading a horoscope, or visiting a fortune-teller.) There were many oracles dotted all over Greece, but the most famous one was the oracle of Apollo – the god of prophecy (seeing into the future) – at Delphi.

On visiting an oracle, you would usually enter an inner sanctuary and ask your question in private. The answer might then come in the form of a babbling spring or a rustling tree. (At Delphi, Apollo spoke through a specially chosen holy woman known as the Pythia who would scream and moan in a trancelike state.) Priests who ran the shrine would then translate the god's 'answers' to you, though you might have to pay them a small fee.

Alexander wanted to ask the oracle about his upcoming Persian adventure, hoping to get an encouraging nod from the gods before he set off. But the oracle at Delphi only operated in summer, and Alex had turned up in the middle of winter. So he went straight to the Pythia's house and tried to drag her to the shrine by force. The poor woman put up quite a fight, but Alexander persisted, and in her frustration she screamed at him:

All she'd meant was that he was stronger than she was, and that she wasn't going to put up a fight. But Alexander decided to take her words as an official announcement from the oracle itself!

Thanks, Mum

On the whole, things seemed to be looking up for Alex, but he was still worried about what was going on at Pella while he was away from the court. Luckily, his mum was there to sort things out for him.

October 335 BC

Dearest Alex,
Don't worry, sweetie, You can sleep easier in
your bed tonight. I've had little Caranus
murdered... along with his sister and their
mother too. (In for a penny, in for a pound,
that's what I say.) So now you can
concentrate on what's important: butchering
all those rebels.
Lots of love and kisses to my darling boy,
   Mumsie x x x

No doubt Olympias was only too pleased to get her
revenge on the woman who'd replaced her in Philip's
affections, but the cruelty of the murders shocked
many people – including, according to some stories,
Alexander himself.

Alexander's Secret Diary
October 335 BC

I feel a tiny bit queasy, to be
honest. Of course, it makes things
much simpler with Caranus out of
the way. But was it really
necessary to be quite so...er...
thorough?
   Oh well, I suppose Mum knows best.

Alex proves his point

Despite the renewed agreement at Corinth, Alexander soon faced another rebellion, and this time the trouble came from the ancient seven-gated city of Thebes, which Philip had worked hard to bring under control. Believing Alexander to be occupied with rebellions in the north, the Thebans now took their chance and claimed independence from the Corinthian League. Everyone who was opposed to Macedonian rule secretly supported the Theban rebellion, and before long, the city was receiving weapons from Athens and gold from the King of Persia.

Alex knew he had to act quickly and decisively, so he marched his army 250 miles over mountainous territory to reach the city walls in just 13 days. (This came as a big shock to the Thebans, who thought it would take him a month or more.) Then he issued a final proclamation:

57

Well, that was enough to send Alex into a rage, and sealed the fate of the city. Alex's army surrounded Thebes, and after a long siege, eventually smashed through its walls. Then the Macedonians rampaged through the streets, looting, plundering and filling the place with blood. Thebes was one of the most historic cities in Greece, but Alex saw that almost every one of its buildings was razed to the ground. Thousands of soldiers were killed and thousands more civilians sold into slavery. Just to show other cities what would happen to those who rebelled against him, Alex simply blotted Thebes from the face of the earth.

Mind you, Alex's brutal tactics certainly did the trick, because all of a sudden the other Greek city-states became *much* more co-operative...

October 335 BC

Dear Alexander, most wise and rightful King of Macedon, We the Athenian people would like to tell you how we rejoiced to see you safely returned from the north. We'd like to say how much we approve of your just punishment of those nasty Thebans. (They had it coming to them, we've always thought so.) And we'd like to assure you of our continued support for the forthcoming invasion of Asia.

Long may you live and...er... all the best!

Love from everyone at Athens

As Alexander made his way back to Pella, he could breathe a huge sigh of relief. He'd shown the rebellious tribes in the north a thing or two, and he'd terrified the Greek city-states into co-operating with him at last. Now he was ready to take up where his father had left off.

Alexander's Secret Diary
October 335 BC

What a brilliant soldier and statesman I am! To celebrate, I'm going to hold a huge festival in honour of Zeus, with a gigantic banquet in my tent. (I might even get my lyre out.)

And in honour of <u>me</u>, I'm also going to issue a new coin. It'll have my gorgeous, handsome face on one side, and a nice picture of Heracles on the back. And it'll mean that ordinary people will be reminded of me every time they pop down the market for a loaf of bread! Cool!

I can't wait to get to Asia. Everything I've done so far is <u>nothing</u> compared to the fame and glory I'll win over there.

THE GREAT EXPEDITION

Now that Alex had secured his position, it didn't take him long to assemble an invasion force. Of course, there were already a few thousand Macedonian troops in Asia Minor, sent by Philip to prepare the way. Alex's main army would soon join them and it was made up like this:

Alexander's expeditionary force

ALEXANDER: CAPTAIN GENERAL OF THE EXPEDITION. SEEN HERE WITH HIS NEW LION'S-HEAD HELMET.

HEPHAISTION: NOW A YOUNG OFFICER IN THE ARMY.

BUCEPHALAS: ALEX'S BEST FOUR-LEGGED FRIEND.

NEARCHUS AND CLEITUS: TWO MORE OF ALEX'S BOYHOOD FRIENDS.

Like his dad, Alex liked to tell everyone that he was going to invade Asia with a vast 'Greek' army, but in fact it was 90 per cent Macedonian. And although most Greeks *said* they supported Alexander, many states actually hoped that his absence from Greece would give them the chance to stir up trouble. To try to prevent this, Alexander chose his trusted adviser Antipater to look after Macedonia while he was away, and he left him around half of the Macedonian army in case he needed it against rebellious Greek states. So much for the idea of Greek unity!

GREAT TIMES: GREEK MERCENARIES

Despite all the talk of a Greek war against the Persian Empire, quite a few Greeks had actually joined the Persian army to fight as mercenaries. Mercenaries are soldiers who fight only for money, and are willing to fight for another country – even one on the 'enemy' side – as long as they get paid for it. The Great King's fabulous wealth attracted thousands of Greek soldiers into the ranks of his armies, and there were actually more non-Macedonian Greeks in the Persian army than there were in the Greek one!

TA!

Homer, sweet Homer

In the spring of the year 334 BC, Alex's vast army set off into Thrace and on towards the Hellespont, the shortest crossing point between Europe and the coast of Asia Minor, the outer edge of the Persian Empire.

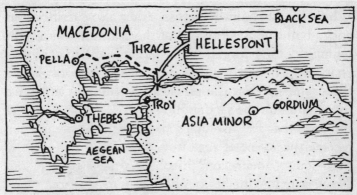

There Alexander packed everything on to about 100 huge ships and, after making sacrifices to the gods for a safe journey, finally set sail. Naturally, Alexander steered the leading ship himself.

Spring 334 BC

Dear Mum,
This is great! Here I am, Captain of the Greeks, leading a mighty army against an Evil Empire. Just what I always dreamed of, and more than Dad ever managed! Now I know how Achilles must have felt when he set sail for the windy plains of Troy.

As soon as I step ashore, I'm going to make a sacrifice to Protesilaus. According to Homer, he was the first Greek soldier to be killed in the war against the Trojans. Hopefully the gods will bring me better luck!

Your darling son,
Ever striving to be the best,
Alex x x

When he was halfway across, Alex also sacrificed an entire bull to Poseidon, god of the sea. (He was a non-swimmer, don't forget, so he didn't want to take any chances.) Then, when they drew near the shore of Asia Minor, he stood at the prow of his ship and threw his spear hard into the sand, telling the gods that he was happy to receive the whole of Asia from them as 'a spear-won prize'. Then, after making his sacrifice to Protesilaus, he set up altars on the shore dedicated to his hero Heracles and to the gods Athena and Zeus.

Next he made a pilgrimage to the ancient city of Troy itself, which was now little more than a ruin. There he and Hephaistion offered more sacrifices at the tombs of Achilles and his loyal friend Patroclus. To honour the Greek heroes from Homer, the two men also competed in a naked running race around the tombs!

Once Alexander had got all that out of his system it was time to get down to business and march east towards the enemy.

A grapple at the Granicus

Meanwhile, in Babylon, at the heart of the Persian Empire, Darius III, the Great King himself, was trying to decide what to do. Among his senior officers was Memnon of Rhodes, a brilliant Greek general who had fallen out with King Philip some years before and gone over to the Persian side to fight as a mercenary...

In the end the Persians decided to confront Alexander before he got far from the coast, though Darius himself chose to stay in Babylon for the time being.

In May the two sides finally met, across the River Granicus...

ALEXANDER WITH 43,000 INFANTRY AND 6,000 CAVALRY

MEMNON WITH 30,000 PERSIAN INFANTRY AND 15,000 CAVALRY

ALEXANDER

PHALANX

ARCHERS

FAST-FLOWING RIVER GRANICUS

MUDDY RIVER BANKS

Alexander's older officers – and especially Parmenio – were wary. They were experienced men and they knew a death trap when they saw one. The Persians had the advantage of higher ground and would surely wait for Alexander to make the first move. The fast-flowing river would be hard to cross and the steep, muddy bank on the far side impossible to climb. Without a doubt, the Macedonians would be cut to pieces.

However, Alexander wasn't easily put off.

HOW ELSE ARE WE GOING TO GAIN GLORY LIKE ACHILLES UNLESS WE OVERCOME IMPOSSIBLE ODDS?

GREAT STORIES: ALEXANDER AND THE CALENDAR
According to one story, some of Alex's officers came up with the excuse that Macedonians didn't usually fight in the month of May, for religious reasons. Alex simply told them that he had used his royal power to change the calendar so it wasn't May any more!

In the end, though, the officers did somehow persuade Alexander to avoid a direct attack across the river. Instead, they waited until nightfall, left their campfires burning to fool the Persians, and snuck away under cover of darkness to a better crossing-point further downstream.

When morning came, Alexander gave the signal and he and Bucephalas led the charge across the river. As Memnon had predicted, the Persians were no match for the Macedonians in open battle, and Alexander soon had his first great victory in Asia under his belt.

Early summer 334 BC

Dear Mum,

Today was great! Hand-to-hand fighting, general mayhem and a spot of butchery. And, of course, I was right in the thick of the action. Mind you, there was one hairy moment when I lost my balance and fell off Bucephalas. A Persian was about to finish me off, but then good old Cleitus arrived and saved the day. Among the prisoners we captured were 2,000 Greek mercenaries. I'm sending them home to work as slaves – that'll serve them right for siding with the enemy.

We also captured loads of Persian loot, and I'm sending it to Athens with a message: 'Alexander sends these spoils from the barbarians who dwell in Asia.' That'll show them how brilliant I am.

Your loving son,
Ever striving to be the best,
Alex x x x

Alexander was soon leading his men further east, 'setting free' many of the towns and cities of Asia Minor. And as his army passed through each important settlement, he left a garrison of soldiers behind to make sure everyone knew who was boss. He also replaced the local Persian rulers – deputies of the Great King known as satraps – with Macedonian officers.

Alexander's Secret Diary
June 334 BC

The only thing that makes me uneasy is the Persian fleet, which has been sighted off the coast of Asia Minor. It's much bigger than ours, and it's now captained by that crafty old devil, Memnon of Rhodes. I don't think we'd stand a chance in a naval battle.

Luckily I've had an absolutely brilliant idea. (Where on earth do I get them from?) Instead of fighting the Persian fleet at sea, I'm going to fight it on land. (I've always preferred to keep my feet dry!) I'll just use my army to capture every single harbour along the coast of Asia Minor - it'll only take a year or so. Then the Persian fleet will have nowhere to pick up supplies and will be forced to surrender.

> And I'm sending my own navy home. We won't be needing them any more, and it'll make the army fight better if they know they've no way back.

Many of the coastal cities surrendered to the Macedonians without a fight, but there were others who locked their gates and resisted. Among them was Halicarnassus, where Memnon of Rhodes soon arrived by sea, along with the Persian fleet. The resulting siege of Halicarnassus held Alexander up for weeks but eventually he captured the city with the help of a local queen named Ada, who'd fallen for his boyish charm and thrown in her lot with him. Together, they forced Memnon to evacuate the city by sea (after burning most of it to the ground) and Alex was then happy to set Ada up as queen, ruling on his behalf. (She was so grateful she even named him as her adopted son.)

HEY, I'M HIS MOTHER, THANK YOU VERY MUCH!

Memnon was soon preparing the Persian fleet for a revenge attack on Greece itself, which would have caused all sorts of problems for Alexander. But then, just as Alex was beginning to wonder whether he'd made a mistake in getting rid of his navy, he heard that Memnon had fallen ill and died suddenly of a fever. As a result, the Persians shelved their plans to invade Greece. For Alex, it was huge stroke of luck, and as he turned his army towards the east, he grew more and more convinced that fortune was on his side.

GREAT STORIES: THE GORDIAN KNOT
Another good omen came at a place called Gordium, where Alex met up with the first batch of reinforcements sent from home. Here, one of the local tourist sights was an antique wagon said to have belonged to the legendary King Midas. (He was the greedy king of Greek mythology who was granted his wish that everything he touch be turned to gold.) The yoke of the wagon was fastened with a huge and complicated knot, and according to a prophecy made by a local oracle, the person who was able to undo the knot was destined to be 'Lord of All Asia'.

Well, this was the sort of thing that Alexander couldn't resist. He was always keen to prove himself in any sort of competition, and he loved anything to do with ancient legends. What's more he was determined to show everyone that he deserved to rule over Asia, so he could hardly pass up a challenge like this.

However, the knot in the thick rope turned out to be extremely tight, with loads of really complicated extra-knotty bits. Many people had failed to untie it. Would Alexander have the patience and skill to succeed where they had failed?

In the end, he was forced to solve the problem in his own way…

It might not have been quite what the oracle had in mind, but it certainly did the trick. At any rate, Alexander was happy to tell everyone that he'd fulfilled the prophecy!

Face to face at last

As Alexander marched his troops east to meet Darius and the Persians, the Great King himself was charging west, and in the end the two armies managed to miss each other completely.

This meant that the first Macedonians Darius stumbled across were the sick and wounded left behind in a makeshift camp, and Darius soon came up with a grisly way to make use of them. First he cut off their hands so they could never fight again, then he sent them on a tour of the Persian army, making sure they got a good look at his fearsome Iranian cavalry, specially brought in for the coming battle. Then Darius sent them to Alexander, to tell him what they'd seen.

When the unfortunate Macedonian prisoners caught up with their own army, they found it in a dreadful state. It had marched 70 miles in two days, only to find that Darius' men had passed them by and now held a good defensive position behind them. The Persians had managed to cut Alex's supply lines, while the Macedonians themselves had been caught in a torrential downpour and were sodden and exhausted. Now they saw what Darius had done to their comrades, and heard vivid first-hand descriptions of the Persian forces. No wonder some of them felt afraid.

It was time for Alexander to say a few words to encourage the men...

Nevertheless, thanks to the speech-making skills he'd learned as a schoolboy, Alex somehow managed to raise morale and prepare his soldiers for another battle.

Here's how the action might have been reported back home…

The Macedonian Mail

Now on sale throughout Greece and Asia Minor
November 333 BC

GREAT KING IN GREAT ESCAPE

and another Great Victory for us Greeks

A special report by our war correspondent, travelling with the Greek forces

Dawn, and the mighty Persian army lies in wait. All along a three-mile front, soldiers crouch behind rows of pointed stakes driven into the far bank of the Pinarus river. In the centre of the Persian lines sits the mighty King Darius himself, mounted high in his golden chariot and surrounded by his bodyguard of crack Iranian troops.

Meanwhile, our own Great King rides up and down the Macedonian lines on his faithful warhorse Bucephalas, searching for the most effective positions for his troops.

7.23 am Suddenly, a gigantic volley of Persian arrows darkens the skies above the battlefield. In response, Alexander leads his cavalry in a headlong charge across the river, scattering the Persian archers.

7.29 am Hampered by the rows of stakes, the Macedonian cavalry somehow scramble up the far bank. Then, determined to confront Darius face to face, our great leader turns his unit sideways and ploughs into the Persian lines.

8.17 am In the carnage of hand-to-hand fighting, and with Alexander only yards away, the horses pulling Darius' chariot go berserk and the Great King himself begins to panic. In the end, Darius abandons his royal chariot and tears away on horseback, leaving behind his royal cloak, his shield and his bow.

Tonight, as the sun goes down on another great victory, Alexander is one step closer to being the new King of Asia.

It might seem a bit weedy of Darius to run away like that, but he knew that the important thing was to stay alive. After all, he could always reorganize his army and fight Alexander another day. And while he still lived, Alexander couldn't really claim to be the King of Asia, no matter how much land he'd conquered.

Nevertheless, Darius' flight soon gave Alex a taste for the high life, because when the Macedonians overran the Persian army's camp, they found it was chock full of gold, silver, weapons and sumptuous oriental tapestries. And when Alex himself arrived he decided to wash off the mud of battle in the Great King's very own bathtub! Then he changed into Darius' splendid bathrobes (though he probably had to roll the sleeves up bit) and entered his pavilion, ablaze with torches. Alexander had all the captured royal gold set out before him and then stretched out on the royal couch for a splendid feast. Turning to his dining companions, he said:

So this *is what it is to be a Great King.*

FLAT TYRE

Alex was still dining after the battle of Issus, when he suddenly heard the sound of wailing and crying coming from a nearby tent. When he went off to investigate he found that among the captured loot was Darius' own family, including his wife, his mother and his children. They were crying because they had seen Darius' empty chariot and thought he was dead.

Luckily for them, Alex knew he would win more respect if he treated them well, so he told them that Darius was still alive and ordered his men to look after them as though they were his own family. In fact, Alex even took to referring to Darius' mother Sisygambis as his 'mum'!

WELL, YOU CAN NEVER HAVE TOO MANY MUMS, CAN YOU?

HUH!

GREAT STORIES: SISYGAMBIS
According to one story, Sisygambis at first mistook Hephaistion for Alex and bowed down before him. This was an awkward moment, but Alex just said, 'Never mind, Mum. He is Alexander too.' (Meaning that Hephaistion – who must have been delighted – was not only his best friend, but more or less an equal.)

Before long, Alex got a letter from Darius, who was anxious to make a deal:

January 332 BC

Dear Alexander,
OK, you won Issus fair and square. But I'm building a bigger army now and next time you won't find it so easy.

Tell you what – I've got tons and tons of gold and I'll pay whatever you want to get my family back. Then I'll let you keep all the land you've won as long as you promise not to come any further.

What do you say?
Yours,
Darius

On the face of it, it seemed a reasonable offer, and one that Alex was afraid his men would want to accept. But Alex didn't want to live *alongside* Darius; he wanted to replace him – as King and Lord of *all* Asia. So, according to one story, he decided not to tell his men about the letter, and instead forged another one that made Darius seem much less reasonable! Encouraged by his men, Alex then wrote a stern reply to Darius, making a great show of telling him who was boss:

January 332 BC

Dear Darius,
How dare you write to me in that tone of voice. Please remember that I'm much greater than you'll ever be, and that everything you think you possess is mine already. (It's not just the missus you lost at the Issus!)

me   you

So if you want anything from me, you'll have to stand and fight for it like a man (if you know how!).
Yours,
Alexander

79

GREAT STORIES: MUMMY'S BOY
According to another story, Darius accused Alex of being nothing more than a naughty little boy, and advised him to go home and sit on his mother's lap where he belonged! To make sure Alex got the point, he even sent him a toy whip and a ball to play with!

A bit of spadework

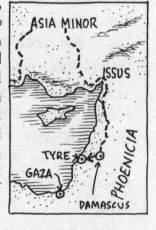

Despite his confidence, Alexander still had plenty to do as he marched his army south from Issus. Before he had complete control of the coastal area known as Phoenicia (modern Israel), he had to deal with several ports that offered vital shelter and supplies for the Persian fleet that still threatened to cut off his own supplies. Chief among these them was the fortress city of Tyre.

The main part of Tyre (known as the New Town) was built behind massive walls on a small island half a mile off the coast where the Old Town still stood. But of course Alexander had no navy, and no catapults capable of doing any damage at that range. The situation looked impossible, but Alexander soon came up with a plan.

YOU MEN WILL SIMPLY HAVE TO KNOCK DOWN OLD TYRE AND USE THE WOOD AND STONES TO BUILD A PLATFORM ALL THE WAY ACROSS. IT ONLY NEEDS TO BE ABOUT 65 METRES WIDE.

DON'T LOOK SO DOWNHEARTED. LAST NIGHT, IN A DREAM, I SAW HERACLES HIMSELF STANDING ON THE WALLS OF TYRE BECKONING TO ME.

I KNOW WHAT IT MEANS! TYRE IS OURS, BUT ONLY AFTER WE HAVE LABOURED LIKE HERACLES HIMSELF FOR OUR VICTORY!

Together with thousands of local men drafted in to help, the Macedonian soldiers soon got down to work … while Alexander helped out by shouting words of encouragement and handing out rewards.

EVER STRIVE TO BE THE BEST, EH LADS?

Meanwhile, the people of New Tyre treated the whole scheme as a great joke that would never work. They even had the cheek to row across in boats, and make fun of Alex's men.

However, they changed their tune after a few weeks, when it became clear that the Macedonians were making progress. As the platform reached halfway across the channel, a deadly struggle between the two sides soon got under way.

1 *The Tyrians sent out eight ships packed with archers, slingers and catapults. Alexander's men, who wore no armour while working, took heavy casualties.*

2 *Along the platform, Alexander rigged up protective screens made from animal hides and canvas.*

3 He also got his men to build two enormous wooden towers from which archers could shoot down into the Tyrian boats.

4 The Tyrians packed a huge ship with firewood and liquid pitch. From the ship's two tall masts hung yardarms carrying cauldrons of burning oil. Then they sent the ship hurtling towards Alexander's wooden towers.

5 Both towers went up in a blazing inferno while from nearby ships Tyrian archers picked off fleeing Macedonians.

6 Tyrian commandos landed on the platform, set fire to it and killed everyone they could find.

At this point, Alexander had some much-needed luck. A number of nearby towns and cities decided to surrender to the Macedonian army and offered Alexander the use of their ships. Now Alexander was able to protect his workforce on the platform with a defensive screen of ships in tight formation, and the enormous platform soon approached the imposing walls of the city.

ROCK-THROWING CATAPULTS MOUNTED ON SHIPS

50-METRE-TALL SIEGE TOWER

BOWLS OF RED-HOT SAND FOR TIPPING ON TO THE ENEMY

ANIMAL HIDES USED TO DEFEND AGAINST MISSILES

ALEXANDER'S PLATFORM

RUBBLE THROWN OVER WALLS TO HAMPER FLOATING RAMS

BATTERING RAM
SUSPENDED
BETWEEN TWO
SHIPS

Eventually, after a long and ferocious struggle, Alexander's men finally succeeded in battering a hole through the walls. They fought their way through a barrage of roof-tiles thrown down by the desperate civilians and finally – after a siege that had lasted seven long months – took hold of the city.

August 332 BC

Dear Mum,
Guess what? I've flattened Tyre! I knew I could do it. It just needed a bit of spadework, that's all. Anyway the men are dead chuffed and have soon forgotten all their whingeing. I'm going to celebrate my brilliant victory with loads of feasting and torchlit processions and whatnot. We'll have running-races, public games, and maybe even a lyre-playing competition. And I'm definitely having that battering ram dedicated to Heracles.

Three cheers for me!
Your brilliant son,
Ever striving...
    Alex x x x

The capture of Tyre was an incredible feat, and the platform Alexander's men built across the sea has never been destroyed. (In fact the modern city of Tyre now stands on its foundations, firmly attached to the mainland.) However, as he'd done at Thebes, Alex decided to deter other towns from resisting him by making a terrible example of the Tyrians. Two thousand soldiers were executed, and thousands more civilians either killed or sold into slavery.

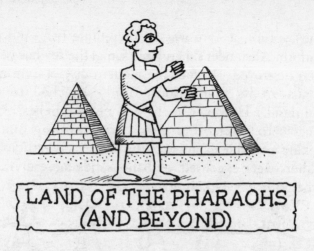

LAND OF THE PHARAOHS (AND BEYOND)

Now that the coastal towns of Phoenicia were secure, Alexander could head towards his next target: Egypt.

The ancient land of pyramids and Pharaohs (not to mention mummies!) had fascinated Alexander ever since he'd read about it as a boy. Now he was determined to make it part of his own kingdom, and he soon ordered his army on a 130-mile forced march south towards the Nile Delta.

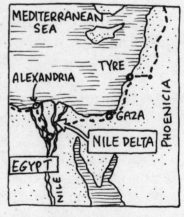

Luckily, Alexander didn't need to do any fighting in Egypt because the Egyptians welcomed him as a liberator. Egypt had once been a proud and independent civilization with its own special religion. But for the past 200 years it had been ruled by the Persians – who had a different religion. So when Alexander arrived and announced he was freeing the Egyptians from Persian oppression, he found that they treated him like a hero.

November 332 BC

Dear Mum,
Guess what? The Egyptians have decided to make me 'Pharaoh', which means King of all Egypt. And even better, it turns out that they believe the Pharaoh is the Son of their Sun-god Ra, so they've been treating me like a god as well as a King. Oh well, I suppose that's Pharaoh nuff! (Geddit?)
Everyone calls me things like 'king of the north and South', 'Son of the Sun' and even 'a god among gods'. Well, it makes sense. After all, you always said there was divine blood in my veins. And I've always known I'm pretty fantastic.
   Anyway, Hephaistion and I have been talking, and we've decided I must try to act like a proper Egyptian Pharaoh. So yesterday I ordered the restoration of two ancient Egyptian temples and made public sacrifices to several Egyptian gods with funny names. (Though I

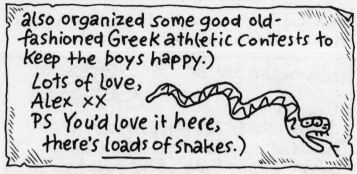

also organized some good old-fashioned Greek athletic contests to keep the boys happy.)
Lots of love,
Alex xx
PS You'd love it here, there's <u>loads</u> of snakes.)

Ask a silly question

While in Egypt, Alexander decided to take a few weeks out for an important mission. He picked a fairly small group of soldiers and set off with them on a 300-mile hike westwards across the wastes of the scorching north-African desert towards a tiny town called Siwah. And it was all because Alexander had an important question for the famous Siwah oracle.

GREAT TIMES: A GREEK ORACLE IN EGYPT?

Although oracles were mainly a Greek thing, there were a few of them spread around neighbouring areas of the ancient world, including Egypt. The Siwah oracle was the oracle of the god Zeus-Ammon, a fusion of two important Greek and Egyptian gods.

No one knows exactly what question Alexander wanted to ask the oracle, but it must have been something quite important. Most people think Alex probably wanted to know whether he really was a god, and not just a mere mortal like the rest of us. All we know for sure is that when he came out of the shrine he was in a very good

90

mood, so it seems as if the priest at Siwah had been wise enough to tell Alex exactly what he wanted to hear!

When he got back to civilization, Alex was brimming with confidence…

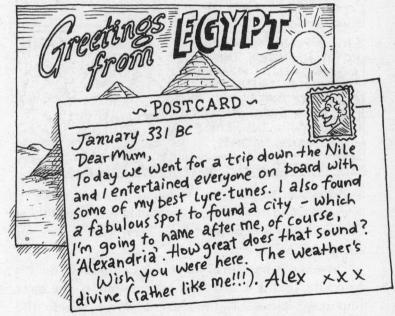

Greetings from EGYPT

~ POSTCARD ~

January 331 BC

Dear Mum,

Today we went for a trip down the Nile and I entertained everyone on board with some of my best lyre-tunes. I also found a fabulous spot to found a city – which I'm going to name after me, of course, 'Alexandria'. How great does that sound? Wish you were here. The weather's divine (rather like me!!!). Alex xxx

Alex had brought loads of architects and engineers with him, but according to one story he was soon giving them his own ideas for the layout of his new city:

Alexander would go on to found dozens of cities all over Asia, and he would call each and every one of them Alexandria! (Which must have been a nightmare for the postman.)

However, it was the Egyptian Alexandria that was his favourite, and it would soon become one of the most important cities of the ancient world, where the glamorous Queen Cleopatra (a descendant of one of Alexander's generals) would one day live in splendour. And even today, more than 2,000 years later, Alexandria is still the second-largest city of Egypt (after Cairo), and still known as 'The Pearl of the Mediterranean'.

A final offer

Alexander was soon ready to lead his army out of Egypt towards new conquests in the east and a final confrontation with Darius. As usual, he left a garrison of Macedonian soldiers behind, but he was happy to leave the running of the country largely in Egyptian hands. This made him popular with the Egyptians themselves, and unlike other parts of his enormous kingdom, Alexander would have little trouble there in future years.

Then, while Alexandria was still under construction, the Macedonians marched back up the Mediterranean coast and then north-east, through modern Syria and into the great plains of Mesopotamia.

Alexander's new objectives were the great cities that lay at the heart of the Persian Empire, the cities whose exotic names had captivated him as a boy: Babylon, Susa, Persepolis and Pasargadae.

Alexander's Secret Diary
Spring 331 BC

I'm sure Hephaistion and the other men wouldn't have minded staying in Egypt and being made a fuss of by those Egyptian girls, but there'll be plenty of time for all that later on. I haven't come all this way just to put my feet up while Darius is in Babylon being the 'Lord of all Asia'. That's _my_ job!

Ever strive to be the best!

Of course, Darius had spent the previous months reorganizing his army and preparing to confront the Macedonians once again if necessary. He planned to stop their advance at the River Tigris, but Alexander managed to cross this, and instead the two armies met in a vast plain near a place called Gaugamela.

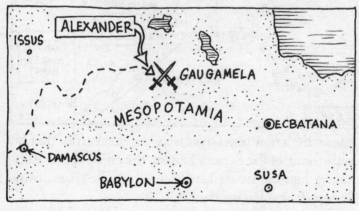

94

On the eve of the battle, Darius' wife – still a prisoner in the Macedonian camp – died while giving birth to Darius' child. Her maid escaped and brought the news to the Great King, who was deeply upset. He even sent Alexander another peace offering.

Autumn 331 BC

Dear Alexander,
OK, this is my final offer. As well as Asia Minor, you can keep all the land you've won west of the Euphrates, including Phoenicia, Syria and Egypt. You're welcome to it, as long as you promise to leave it at that.
Plus you can have 30,000 talents in cash if I can have my family back.
Yours
Darius, Lord of all Asia (except the bit I'm giving to you)

It was a very generous offer, since Darius was basically agreeing to surrender a third of his entire empire. If Alexander had accepted, he could have returned to Macedonia with pride and would certainly have been celebrated for centuries for his great conquests. But for Alexander, it wasn't enough. He wanted the *whole* of Darius' empire and would never be satisfied with anything less.

According to one story, he showed the letter to his general, Parmenio, and asked for his advice:

But Alexander was Alexander, so he wrote back to Darius telling him that just as the earth could not be imagined with two suns, so the continent of Asia was unimaginable with two kings. They would have to fight for it, and he – Alexander – would win.

Five against one

Such a confident reply to Darius' letter was typical, but Alexander may have regretted it in the morning when he went out to survey the Persian army from a nearby ridge. If he'd expected an army like the one he'd defeated at Issus, he was much mistaken.

Alexander spent several hours riding around on Bucephalas, surveying the vast enemy formations. Then he returned to his tent for good hard think. Parmenio visited him at one point and suggested a surprise attack in the middle of the night, but Alexander dismissed this idea, saying that he wanted to win an *honourable* victory with no cheating.

There was no sign of Alexander in the camp the next morning, and in the end Parmenio had to go and rouse him from his bed.

Perhaps Alexander's greatest strength was his knowledge of tactics, and that night in his tent he'd come up with a winning plan…

The Macedonian Mail

now available in hieroglyphs
October 331 BC

ALEXANDER: LORD OF ASIA!

- Barbarian Hordes Crushed In Epic Battle
- Alexander Overcomes Impossible Odds
- Great King Escapes Again

In what was surely one of the greatest battles of all time, King Alexander has achieved a historic victory on behalf of all Greeks. Yesterday he defeated the full force of the mighty Persian army once and for all.

The Great King's army consisted of hundreds of units drawn from every region of the vast Persian Empire, including fearsome cavalry brigades from Bactria and deadly squadrons of scythed chariots. According to some eyewitness reports there were more than half a million men on the battlefield, with the Macedonian army outnumbered by five to one.

Scythed chariots: deadly new weapon

One soldier explained: 'The Persians had spent several days preparing the battlefield by flattening and smoothing the ground for their scythed chariots, but we were also well prepared. Our ranks stood their ground until the chariots were almost upon us, then stepped aside at the last moment, allowing them to pass through.'

When General Parmenio's cavalry attacked on the left, Persian forces were drawn away from the centre, while the Macedonian infantry moved forward steadily, each phalanx bristling with deadly sarissas. Then, when a gap opened up in the Persian lines, King Alexander himself led the charge against it, and headed straight for the Great King's chariot. Darius soon became cut off from his men and fled from the field. Hours later his army had been destroyed.

Alexander is already King of Macedon, Leader of Greece, Overlord of Asia Minor and Pharaoh of Egypt. Now he is also King and Lord of All Asia.

Alexander, we salute you!

October 331 BC

Dear Mum,
Is that Darius scared of me or what? That's the <u>second</u> time he's run away in the middle of a battle. I would have chased after him too, but I had to go and help out Parmenio who was in spot of trouble on the left-wing.

I really am rather fantastic, aren't I? I mean even compared with Achilles and Heracles and all those chaps. I might be on the small side, but when it comes to actual <u>greatness</u> I reckon I'm even greater than they were!

Yup, that oracle was dead right. There's <u>definitely</u> something rather godlike about me.

Your son,
Ever striving...
(and mostly succeeding!)
Alex xx

me

BY THE RIVERS OF BABYLON

Darius' reputation as Great King was beginning to lose its shine, but Alexander was quickly winning a name for himself throughout the empire. And as he marched his army further east he found many great cities throwing their gates open and surrendering to him as their conqueror. Among them was one of the most glorious in the whole of the ancient world: Babylon.

ALEXANDER LEADS HIS ARMY INTO THE CITY

THE MASSIVE ISHTAR GATE IS THROWN OPEN TO RECEIVE HIM

THE RIVER EUPHRATES BISECTS THE CITY AS DOES THE GREAT PROCESSIONAL WAY

THE FAMOUS HANGING GARDENS OF BABYLON, BUILT BY AN ASSYRIAN KING FOR HIS IRANIAN WIFE, AND LATER KNOWN AS ONE OF THE SEVEN ANCIENT WONDERS OF THE WORLD

CROWDS ON PARAPET WALLS CHEER AND SHOWER ROSES ON THEIR CONQUEROR

MUD-BRICK OUTER WALLS: 15 MILES LONG ON EACH SIDE AND WIDE ENOUGH FOR TWO FOUR-HORSED CHARIOTS TO RIDE ABREAST ON THEM

Alexander decided that his men needed a rest and he made up his mind to give them a month's leave that they would never forget. And while his men enjoyed themselves, Alexander spent his time studying Babylonian astrology. (Perhaps he was hoping for some more good omens.)

Treasure beyond measure

Next stop was Susa, 375 miles south-east of Babylon, and another of the Great King's palatial cities.

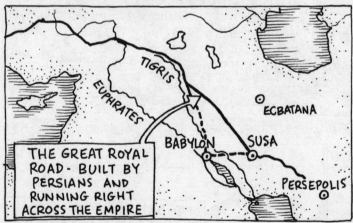

This time, the local satrap came out to greet Alexander as he made his way along the Royal Road. With him, he brought gifts including a herd of camels and a dozen elephants. (Gradually the Macedonian army was beginning to look more like a travelling zoo.) Then he formally surrendered the city and offered to give Alexander a guided tour of the Royal Palace and its fabulous treasury.

Inside, Alexander found riches that even he could never have dreamed of. As well as a fabulous hoard of gold and silver coins, there were piles and piles of gold plate and jewellery, not to mention roll after roll of the finest ancient tapestries and enormous rooms full of other luxurious furnishings. And in the middle of it all was the Great King's legendary throne, with its splendid golden canopy.

Alexander's first act after inspecting his newly won fortune was to seat himself in the Great King's throne. It wasn't just that he wanted to take the weight off his sandals after all that marching. It was more important than that. He wanted to make an important symbolic gesture to show the world that he – Alexander – was the new Great King.

Unfortunately, Alex had forgotten that he wasn't nearly as tall as Darius...

Alexander's Secret Diary
November 331 BC

Right, that's the last time I sit on any Persian thrones, unless I get someone to make the necessary adjustments first. I looked a right idiot! Still, as Hephaistion says, things aren't going too badly. All that dosh should make things easier and reinforcements have now arrived from Greece, so the army's up to full strength. (A good job, too, as we lost quite a few men at Gaugamela.)

But the news from home isn't good. Antipater's having trouble keeping the city-states in line, though he reckons he's won a 'great' victory at a place called Megalopolis. (Yeah, right. It's <u>Me</u> who's winning the

great battles.) To be honest, I'm
losing interest in Macedonia. It
seems so far away now, it's hard to
care. Let Antipater deal with it. I'm
sure Mum'll be glad to help.

GREAT STORIES: THE BATTLE OF MICE
According to one story, Alexander wrote to
Antipater telling him that compared to his own
magnificent victory at Gaugamela, the battle at
Megalopolis was only a 'battle among mice'!

A wild night

A few hundred miles further to the east, at the very heart
of Persia itself, lay the holy city of Persepolis, the religious
capital of the Persian Empire and the traditional burial
place of its kings. This was Alexander's next port of call,
and though he had a spot of bother on the way from a
small army of Persian guerrillas rolling stones down on his
army from the top of a mountain pass...

...the Macedonian army got there in one piece.

Inside, they found yet more treasure lying there for the taking – piles and piles of it. In fact, in order to transport it westwards Alexander had to use every single pack animal in his army, as well as more than 3,000 extra camels!

CARRYING ALL THIS LOOSE CHANGE – IT'S ENOUGH TO GIVE YOU THE HUMP!

At Babylon and Susa, the Macedonian soldiers had been relatively well behaved. They'd had a good time, for sure, but they'd treated their hosts with respect. Above all, Alexander had given them strict instructions not to trash the place.

In Persepolis, however, things were different. This time Alexander decided to give his men free reign to act as they liked, and unfortunately they chose to tear through the city in a terrifying spree of burning, looting and killing.

No one really knows why Alex decided to destroy Persepolis – another dodgy episode in his career. Perhaps he felt it would be a rallying point for Persian resistance. Perhaps he wanted to claim revenge for the burning of Athens during the Persian Wars. Whatever the reason, it certainly cost Alexander a lot of respect among his new subjects. Even the great ancient palace of Xerxes was burnt to the ground, and it may have been Alexander himself who lit the match. At first Alexander had ordered the palace to be preserved as a museum, but according to one story he got drunk at a great feast and was led astray by Thais, the Athenian girlfriend of one of his officers.

Alexander's Secret Diary
December 331 BC

Woke up this morning with a very sore head and a broken lyre round my neck. And now I can't get this burning smell out of my nostrils.

Don't remember too much about last night, but I think we got a bit carried away. And all because of that Thais girl. One minute she's saying how boring the evening is without a few fireworks. Next she's fluttering her eyelashes and suggesting we burn the palace down.

I dread to think what Aristotle would say. We Greeks aren't meant to overdo the plonk and lose our heads. 'All things in moderation' — he was always banging on about that.

Oh well, you've got to let off a bit of steam now and then, that's what I say!

LORD OF ALL ASIA

Alexander soon moved on from the heat of Persepolis, doubling back on himself slightly and pushing his army north-west through the mountains of what is now known as Iran to a place called Ecbatana. There he installed General Parmenio – now 70 years old – as local satrap. He also stationed a number of troops in Ecbatana, and sent quite a few home to Greece. He wanted to slim down his army for the tough, mountainous territory that lay ahead.

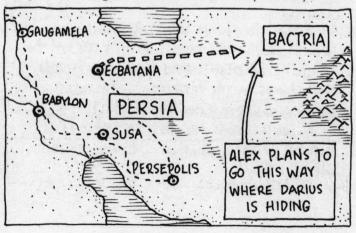

GAUGAMELA

BACTRIA

ECBATANA

BABYLON

PERSIA

SUSA

PERSEPOLIS

ALEX PLANS TO GO THIS WAY WHERE DARIUS IS HIDING

Alex still hoped to catch his archenemy Darius alive, so that he could force him to step down and officially hand his empire over. That way, people would see Alex as a lawful successor to Darius, not just a brutal war-mongering tyrant.

However, Alex's hopes were soon dashed when he received word that Darius had been deposed by one of his own generals – a man called Bessus who had commanded a Persian cavalry wing at Gaugamela. Bessus had now proclaimed himself Great King, and boasted that Darius was his prisoner.

In response, Alexander chose 500 of his toughest men and persuaded them to make an all-night dash across the Iranian desert in order to catch up with Bessus and 'rescue' Darius.

They made the crossing in double-quick time, and almost caught Bessus napping. However, all they found at his hastily abandoned campsite was a single wagon – and from inside it came some very strange moaning noises.

So he could get away from Alexander more quickly on horseback, Bessus had run his prisoner through with a javelin and left him for dead. Alexander ordered his men to fetch water for Darius, but it was too late. The once Great King had breathed his last.

> ### Alexander's Secret Diary
> #### July 330 BC
> Damn and blast! Now there's no chance of anyone handing the throne to me, and I'll have to fight for it all over again.
>
> Hephaistion says the only thing to do is act like Darius' real successor and chase after Bessus as though I were taking revenge on Darius'

behalf. (I'll chase him to the ends of the earth if necessary!)

I've just got to persuade people that I'm a world-class statesman and Bessus is just a thug. Think I'll start by giving Darius a grand state funeral in Persepolis (er...what's left of it). 'He was a noble enemy and shall be treated as he deserves' etc etc. That should win a few Persian hearts and minds.

Naturally, I'm doing my best to wear a long face and look as if I'm mourning the loss of my best friend. And I'm going to spread the rumour that Darius gave me his blessing with his dying breath. (Where do I get these brilliant ideas?)

Unfortunately for Alexander, the death of Darius soon led to other rumours spreading through the Macedonian camp...

WE'RE GOING HOME! THAT'S WHAT I'VE HEARD. WE'LL SOON BE SEEING OUR FAMILIES AGAIN!

It started off as little more than wishful thinking on the part of soldiers who were weary of marching across thousands of miles of desert. They'd been away for four years now, and not only had they taken over the capital cities of the Persian Empire but now they'd actually seen off King Darius himself. Why shouldn't they go home for a well-earned rest? That's what they thought, and the idea spread so fast that before you could say 'Alexandropolis' it had become an established fact among the troops, even though Alexander himself knew nothing about it.

> **August 330 BC**
>
> Dear Mum,
> You'll never believe it, but this morning I woke to the sound of wagons being packed. The men were getting ready to head home! I had to make the speech of my life to convince them to stay.
>
> You should have seen me, Mum, I was great! I managed to get the tears flowing down my cheeks as I told them they were abandoning their leader 'in the mid-course of his glory'. (Nice phrase, that one.)
>
> 'We stand on the very threshold of victory...' I said. 'And you're leaving me?' Lots of stuff like that – I really laid it on thick.
>
> In the end I got them cheering and they decided to stick with me.

The emperor's clothes

As time went by, Alexander found that he needed his speech-making skills more and more often, because he wasn't getting on with his officers as well as he once did. Here's why...

For a while now, Alex had started to dress a bit strangely, copying various Persian fashions. First he'd tried out Darius' royal headband, and then put on some fancy oriental robes as well – not to mention the eyeliner and mascara that were all the rage among Persian men. (Mind you, he drew the line at wearing *trousers*, a Persian invention that even Alex considered a bit too weird!) Soon, Alex was encouraging his friends to wear Persian clothes and even started decking out the Macedonian horses in ornate Persian harnesses!

What was going on?

Well, Alexander realized that he had a huge empire to govern, stretching over thousands and thousands of miles. There was no way he had enough Macedonian troops to cover all of it, and if he was ever going to win enough support among the Persians for them to let him rule them peacefully, he was going to have to meet them halfway. And if they expected their king to act like a Persian, then that's just what he'd have to do. (Mind you, there's not much doubt that Alexander also quite liked the look of himself in Darius' fancy gear. And it's even been suggested that one reason he took to wearing Persian shoes – which had raised heels – was just so he'd look a bit taller!)

The new fashion at court was fine with most of Alexander's close friends, but the older officers who'd once fought for King Philip were a conservative bunch and preferred to stick to the traditional Macedonian way of doing things. According to them it ought to be the Persians who adopted *their* ways, not the other way round.

TSK-TSK. IT WAS NEVER LIKE THIS IN OUR DAY!

To keep the officers happy in true Macedonian style, and to try to take their minds of their growing list of complaints, Alex began to organize more and more feasts and all-night drinking parties. But he also encouraged his soldiers to find Persian girlfriends and marry them.

He was hoping that he'd be able to persuade them to forget about their homes in Macedonia and think of the Persian campaign as a permanent way of life.

Alexander's Secret Diary
August 330 BC

I haven't said anything to the men, but I'm actually beginning to wonder if I <u>ever</u> really want to return to Macedonia. It'd be nice to see Mum, but apart from that I can't think of a single reason to go back. Hephaistion reckons I could rule my empire from Babylon instead of Pella. It's much more central, after all (and far less boring).

Anyway, this is no time for thinking about settling down <u>anywhere</u>. Bessus has set up his HQ in Bactria, further to the east, and we've <u>got</u> to track him down. Personally, I can't wait for more adventures, but the men aren't going to like it.

THE GOING GETS TOUGH

Bactria lay in the remote north-eastern corner of the Persian Empire, in the area known today as Afghanistan, and it was a horribly mountainous place that caused Alex all sorts of problems. Bessus was crafty enough not to fight him in a head-on battle – after all, he'd already seen what Alex was capable of in *that* situation. Instead, he used the mountains to his advantage, forcing the Macedonians into dangerous passes and then attacking them with hit-and-run raids.

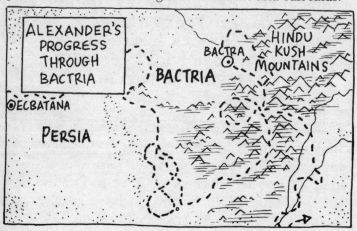

ALEXANDER'S
PROGRESS
THROUGH
BACTRIA

⊙ECBATANA

PERSIA

BACTRIA

BACTRA ⊙

HINDU KUSH MOUNTAINS

Worse still, the Macedonians had to keep doubling back on themselves to crush rebellions in their rear. No sooner would they move on again than local tribesmen would emerge from the mountain mists and slaughter the Macedonian garrisons that had been left behind. Or else local satraps who had surrendered to Alex would rise up in revolt as soon as he'd left the scene.

With many men suffering from frostbite, snow-blindness, altitude sickness and sore feet, conquering Bactria was an extremely frustrating business for the Macedonians, and it would take them more than a year. It's not surprising that the situation soon began to play on Alexander's nerves...

The plots thicken

As complaints from among the ranks grew more frequent by the day Alexander became more and more worried about the continued loyalty of his men. Were they plotting against him? Was he about to be betrayed?

Not for the first or the last time, worries like these caused him to act ruthlessly, and one of those next to pay the price was General Parmenio, now serving as the local ruler at Ecbatana in western Persia. Parmenio was a hugely respected officer in the Macedonian army – one of the old-guard who'd been fighting battles for King Philip when Alexander was still in his nappies. Parmenio had recently made it clear to everyone that he didn't think much of Alexander's new Persian ways and Alex began to think he might be better off without him. But Parmenio was popular with the men, so Alex couldn't just have him arrested for no reason. However, he soon saw a chance to get rid of Parmenio through his much less popular son, a boastful and bigheaded man named Philotas.

One day Philotas was approached by a young man, who told of a rumour he'd heard concerning a plot to kill Alexander. Philotas promised the man he would

warn Alexander, but for some reason he didn't, and when Alexander eventually heard about it, he saw his chance. He had Philotas arrested, and then tortured until he 'confessed' to plotting with his father against Alexander. Sentence was soon passed and Philotas (among others) was stoned to death. Then Alexander sent two of his men on a special mission:

1 Carrying a letter for Parmenio they sped across the desert on racing camels, reaching Ecbatana before Parmenio had a chance to hear news of his son's fate.

2 While Parmenio was still opening the letter – which turned out to be his own death warrant – they hacked him to pieces. They even sent his head back to Alexander as proof that they'd carried out their task.

Alexander's Secret Diary
September 330 BC

It seems harsh, I know. Parmenio was a nice old boy really, but he did have some rather old-fashioned ideas. When you're in my position, you have to make tough decisions like that. (It's not easy being great, you know.)

Unfortunately, bumping off his senior officers did little to make things any easier for Alex, since it only stirred up more resentment and suspicion among the ordinary soldiers. According to one story, Alex became so worried about what his men were thinking that he soon came up with a sneaky plan to find out.

• First he encouraged them to write home to their families in Macedonia by telling them that this would be one of the last chances they'd have before the territory got so rough and mountainous that letters might not get through.

• Then he despatched the huge mound of letters with his own couriers.

• After they'd gone a little way, he recalled them and told them to deliver all the post to his own tent.

• There he stayed up all night reading the letters, to see what his men were saying about him!

Dear mum, Alexander is a short, annoying, big-headed lunatic who is going to

Anyone who had complained or said bad things about Alex in their letters soon found themselves attached to a special new unit in the Macedonian army, a unit that Alex reserved for only the most dangerous and hopeless missions.

Alexander's Secret Diary
October 330 BC

Thanks to my cunning plan I've managed to weed out a few treacherous types. Trouble is, we're also taking a lot of casualties in Bactria, and I'm running short of men now. So I've decided to do something really brave and daring (as well as downright brilliant, if I do say so myself). I'm going to recruit thousands of Persian troops from the lands I've already conquered. After all, I'm their Great King now, and they can jolly well fight for me. (And if my Macedonian men don't like it, that's just tough.)

Alex loses his cool

Gradually Bessus retreated further and further north, and Alex was forced to chase him beyond Bactria into the land of Sogdiana (known today as Uzbekistan and Tajikistan). This was unknown territory on the very furthest northern reaches of the Persian Empire.

The local Sogdian ruler, a man known as Spitamenes, didn't fancy a run-in with the Macedonians so he captured Bessus and handed him over to Alex as part of a peace deal. (Alex could never forgive Bessus for his treatment of Darius, and had him executed.) However, Spitamenes soon changed his mind about wanting to be friends, and before long the Macedonians (together with the Persian recruits now fighting alongside them) were marching up and down ever more remote regions in hot pursuit of yet *another* enemy.

Spitamenes used similar tactics to Bessus, but he also teamed up with horsemen from the warlike tribes who lived in the vast plains to the north. Altogether, he proved a very tricky opponent, and the search for him dragged on and on – even after Alexander had divided his army into five separate groups to cover more ground.

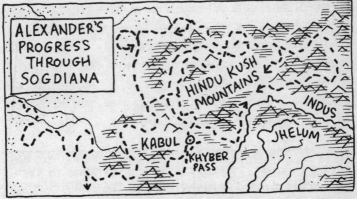

Meanwhile, the atmosphere among the Macedonians was getting worse by the day and Alexander's touchiness about his men's loyalty soon got the better of him once again. One night, during a late-night dinner party, Alex got drunk and decided to make a speech.

Most of the Macedonians were too frightened of Alexander to disagree. They just kept their thoughts to themselves and toasted his health. But Alexander's trusted friend Cleitus, the man who'd saved his life at the Granicus, just wasn't prepared to go along with this. He knew how fed up the men really were, and he thought they had good reason. So he stood up and made a speech of his own.

That was enough for Alexander, who completely lost his temper and reached for the nearest weapon to hand.

Within seconds, fists were flying and the two men were going at each other hammer and tongs, while their friends did their best to separate them. In the end it was Alex who finished it by reaching for another weapon – a much deadlier one this time.

As soon as he saw what he'd done, Alex froze, full of remorse. He realized immediately that he'd made a terrible, terrible mistake – and, what was worse, *everyone had seen him do it!*

After a few moments of dreadful silence in which nobody knew *where* to look, Alex adopted a tried and tested method of dealing with awkward situations: he ran off to his tent for a sulk!

Alexander's Secret Diary
November 328 BC

Oh blimey, I've really put my foot in it now. Everyone's totally horrified and I can't blame them, really. After all, I'm not supposed to blow my top like that, it's completely uncool! I know what Aristotle would say, I can hear him now. 'How can you claim to govern a great empire if you can't even govern yourself?' Even Hephaistion's a bit miffed.

What am I going to do? I'm certainly not coming out of my tent till things have blown over a bit. I think I'll just stay put and practise on my lyre.

In fact, for the next few days Alexander refused to eat and told everyone he was starving himself to death because he felt so bad about what had happened. In the end, his tactics worked, because although his men were unhappy with Alex, they also needed him to get them home. So, eventually, they came to his tent and begged him to come out, telling him they didn't want to be left leaderless in such a remote and dangerous region. They also told him that as King and Lord of All Asia (not to mention son of god) and he was above all ordinary laws, and that he shouldn't worry *too* much about killing Cleitus. In a way, they said, it was only right that Cleitus should be put to death for criticizing Alexander. All in all, everyone was prepared to put the incident behind them, if only Alex would come out of his tent and lead them on to further victories. It must have been music to Alex's ears!

Top of the world

Eventually, after two years' tramping around the mountains of Sogdiana, the Macedonians received a bit of good news from the northern tribesmen. They'd decided to betray Spitamenes (just as he'd betrayed Bessus, and

Bessus had betrayed Darius), and they even had the courtesy to send Spitamenes' head as a peace offering.

With that, Alex decided he'd gone far enough in a northerly direction, and to prove his point, he founded a fortified city in the north of Sogdiana called 'Alexandria-the-Furthest'.

However, before he could leave Sogdiana altogether, he still had to deal with one more rebellious local leader called Oxyartes. Together with 30,000 men, and enough supplies for a two-year siege, he'd holed himself up in a high mountain stronghold known as the Sogdian Rock. This was at the top of a sheer cliff face, and Oxyartes was convinced it was impregnable. In fact he was *so* sure that he and his men jeered at the Macedonians, telling them that if they wanted to capture the rock they would first have to learn how to fly!

Well, of course, that was like a red rag to a bull and Alex was soon picking 300 men for a very special mission. Kitted out with ropes, iron wedges to drive into the rock-face, and no doubt some *very* stout sandals, these men were ordered to climb the cliff face on the far side of Oxyartes' fortress where they would be hidden from view. It was a tough climb, by any standards, and several of the men plunged to their deaths. But by the morning the survivors stood high on the summit of the Sogdian rock, looking down into Oxyartes' camp. As the sun rose, they each took out a white sheet that Alex had asked them to carry with them and waved it in the wind. Oxyartes took one look and was so surprised by these 'winged-men' that he surrendered his fortress on the spot!

The Macedonians then moved in and no doubt celebrated their victory with much wining and dining. For Alex, it was time to take stock...

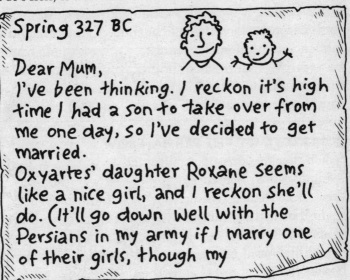

Spring 327 BC

Dear Mum,
I've been thinking. I reckon it's high time I had a son to take over from me one day, so I've decided to get married.
Oxyartes' daughter Roxane seems like a nice girl, and I reckon she'll do. (It'll go down well with the Persians in my army if I marry one of their girls, though my

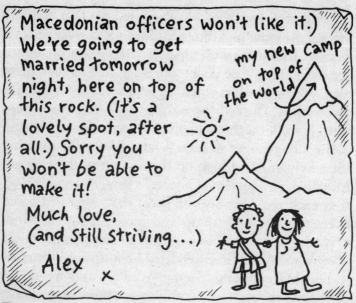

Bow-wow-wow

Once the hastily organized wedding was over, Alex soon got his army back on the march, and – perhaps under the influence of his new Persian wife – it wasn't long before he was trying to introduce another exotic oriental custom that he rather liked the look of. This was a little matter of getting everyone to grovel on the ground in front of him!

GREAT TIMES: THE PERSIAN BOW

For the Persians, it was normal to greet anyone important by bowing before them. It was just a way of acknowledging the person's rank. (And, of course, the Great King himself would expect a bow from absolutely everyone.) However, Greeks never usually bowed before any mere mortal, even if he was a king, but only before their gods.

So when Alexander announced that he'd like all his Macedonian officers to come to a drinking-party and bow down before him as Great King, many of them were horrified. Alex had promised to give them a kiss in return, a traditional Greek sign of equality, but that didn't cut any ice with the older Macedonians. For them, bowing to Alexander would be downright humiliating, as well as offensive to their gods. However, they all knew what happened to people who didn't go along with Alexander's new ideas, so most of them just swallowed their pride and made a quick bow before sidling off.

There was one person, however, who refused outright. This was Aristotle's nephew Callisthenes, one of the historians who'd been brought along on the trip, and a popular chap in the army. In the past, he'd supported Alexander against the older Macedonian fuddy-duddies, but this was a step too far.

129

Well, you couldn't be as cheeky as *that* to Alexander and hope to get away with it, no matter whose nephew you were. Alexander managed to resist the temptation to kill Callisthenes on the spot, but he soon had him arrested on trumped-up charges, and a short while later he was sentenced to death. According to some stories, Callisthenes was simply hanged. According to others, he was dragged along behind the Macedonian army in a cage until he died of starvation.

TO THE ENDS OF THE EARTH

Now that Darius, Bessus and Spitamenes were all dead, Alexander was clearly in charge across virtually the whole of the Persian Empire. But if anyone in his army thought he was planning to go home and live a quiet life with his new wife Roxane, they soon had another think coming.

Before the year was out Alexander was marching his army – now numbering around 100,000 – further east across the vast mountain range of the Hindu Kush (on the border between modern Afghanistan and Pakistan). And he was leading them towards what he imagined was the very edge of the world itself.

Alexander's Secret Diary
Autumn 327 BC

I've told my men we're not stopping till we reach the Ocean at the End of the World. ⟶

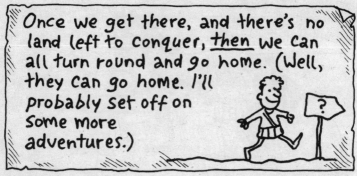

Once we get there, and there's no land left to conquer, then we can all turn round and go home. (Well, they can go home. I'll probably set off on some more adventures.)

Unfortunately, Alexander only had a very hazy idea about the geography of the land he and his men were now travelling through, and he was relying on something Aristotle had told him at school. He'd said that you'd be able to see the Ocean at the End of the World as you looked east from the summit of the Hindu Kush mountain range. That's because he thought the world looked like this:

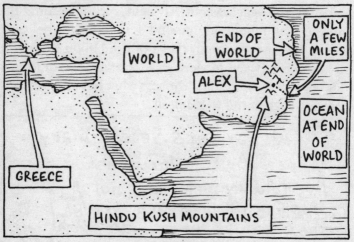

Alexander had repeated this idea over and over again to his men, and as they wound their way up the steep mountains they must have thought they'd soon be having a lovely holiday by the beach before heading home.

But when they got to the top there wasn't the slightest sign of an ocean, only dry land stretching all the way to the horizon. Alexander didn't know it yet, but the Ocean at the End of the World (known to us as the Indian Ocean) was over 1,000 miles away. That's because the world really looks more like this:

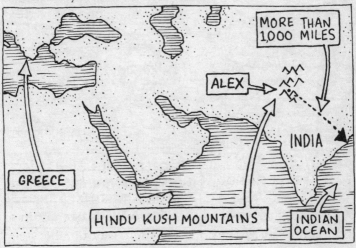

Magical mystery tour

Between the Macedonian army and the ocean Alexander was looking for lay the land known as India. The Greeks had heard of India – though they hadn't realized quite how big it was! – and for them it was a place surrounded in myth and fable. Heracles was supposed to have gone there on his travels, and so was the god Dionysus. Not surprisingly, Alex wanted to follow in their footsteps and somehow he persuaded his men to go on. Perhaps he appealed to their curiosity by reminding them of the various travellers' tales that had described India as a land full of weird and wonderful creatures...

Of course, the Macedonians didn't find anything *quite* like that, though they did find plenty of fairly strange-looking animals…

…as well as weather conditions that they'd never encountered before, including torrential monsoon rains when it poured constantly for weeks on end. Alexander's men had crossed burning deserts and icy mountains, but nothing had quite prepared them for India. Soaked to the skin, they had to trudge on through miles of stinking swamps swarming with malaria-carrying mosquitoes, while their weapons rusted in the damp air, and their clothes rotted in the heat. Many of them suffered from foot-rot, prickly heat and dysentery.

To top it all off, they also had to fight one of the fiercest battles in the whole campaign. This was against Porus, a local Indian king who refused to submit to Alexander. Other kings had surrendered to Alex straight away, but Porus had good reason to be defiant, because he commanded possibly the most fearsome-looking army that Alexander ever met:

The battle against Porus took place on the muddy banks of the River Jhelum, swollen with the monsoon rains, and it turned out to be a bloodbath as well as a mudbath. Many Macedonians were trampled to death by the elephants, while others were impaled on their tusks. Some were simply picked up in their huge trunks and dashed to the ground while the elephants made terrifying trumpeting noises.

Eventually, however, Alexander's men managed to get the better of the elephant army. First they began to pick off the drivers with arrows or javelins and then, hacking at the poor animals' feet and trunks, they drove them into a frenzy so that they began to trample the Indian soldiers on their own side.

That swung things in Alexander's favour, and it wasn't long before his army had chalked up one more great victory. However, it was a victory that cost many lives, including one that was especially dear to Alex.

tear stains →

May 326 BC

Dear Mum,
You'll never guess what's happened.
Bucephalas is dead! My lovely horse!
We were just seeing off the last
of the elephants when Porus' son
appeared out of nowhere, with his
sabre flashing. Good old Bucephalas
reared up at his elephant and took a

horrible wound across the tummy.
He struggled on till the end of the
battle, and I thought he might be
OK. But when I went to give him his
hay this morning, he'd passed away
in his sleep.

He was 30 years old, and he's been
everywhere with me. Things just
won't be the same without him.
I've decided to found a city on the
banks of the River Jhelum, and I'm
going to name it Bucephala.
Lots of love,
Alex x x
PS It's no good offering to buy me
another horse. It won't be the same!
PPS Boo-hoo!

The final frontier

Alex wasn't one for sitting around moping, and as far as
he was concerned the great victory over Porus was just
the beginning of his campaign in India. He planned to
push on to the ocean, however long it took, crossing
every river and fighting every
tribe on the way. He was the
greatest conqueror the world
had ever seen and he wasn't
stopping now, even though
the captured King Porus had
probably told him the truth
about how far away the
ocean really was...

SHHH! DON'T TELL THE
OTHERS!

However, Alexander's army had finally had enough. They were fed up with marching day after day in sodden, rotting clothes and sleeping in hammocks hung from trees to avoid being bitten by snakes. They were fed up with hearing the air whining with mosquitoes and rumours of savage tribes ahead of them. Above all, they were fed up with Alexander and his never-ending enthusiasm for pushing onwards, whatever the obstacles. They certainly no longer believed him when he told them, as he always did, that they would find the Ocean over the next hill.

The army had finally come to see that Alexander would never be satisfied, and that he had no intention of ever going home. Conquering new land had become a way of life for him. He wasn't interested in looking after the empire he'd already won, he just wanted to keep winning more.

Many of the men in the army had been recruited along the way, but quite a few of the original expeditionary force remained as well. Over the eight years since they'd set out, they'd marched with Alexander for over 17,000 miles!

Not surprisingly, they wanted to go home, see their families and put their feet up.

The last straw came when they reached yet another wide river, and heard stories of an Indian tribe waiting for them on the other side with no fewer than 4,000 fighting elephants. Alex was all ready for another big scrap, but the army simply threw down their weapons and refused to cross the river.

Clearly they meant business, so Alex cleared his throat and made one of his all-time greatest speeches.

Unfortunately, Alex's speech fell completely flat. His men had heard it all before a thousand times, and they just didn't believe a word of it any more. One of them – a brave soldier called Coenus – even made his own speech, explaining to Alexander that there was one thing above all else that a successful man ought to know: *when to stop*.

Alexander soon saw that he was facing a full-scale mutiny. Naturally, he tried sulking in his tent for two days, but even that wasn't going to wash this time, and all he could hear from under his bedclothes were the sounds of the army packing everything for the return journey. In the end, he just had to face the fact that for once in his life he *wasn't* going to get his way, and reluctantly he agreed to head for home. His conquests had finally come to an end.

Alexander's Secret Diary
June 326 BC

Damn and blast it! I might have known I couldn't rely on that ragbag of an army. Call themselves soldiers? Wimping out after a mere 17,000 miles. It's pathetic!
What's the point of being great like me if you're surrounded by a load of weeds and softies who can't even fight their way across a single continent without getting homesick?
   Anyway, I can't let people think

> I've caved in, so I've arranged for my soothsayer to find some ill-omens for the journey ahead. That way I can just say that the gods were against us going any further, and blame the whole thing on them. (Lucky I'm still having those great ideas!)

Before turning back for the return journey, the Macedonians set up 12 enormous statues of the Greek gods on the banks of the river.

GREAT STORIES
According to one story the Macedonians also built enormous fortifications, complete with extra-gigantic furniture – just to make people think that the men who had built them were a race of giants! (Wonder whose idea *that* was.)

Finally, to mark the outer limits of Alexander's empire, they set up a huge brass obelisk bearing one simple message:

ALEXANDER STOPPED HERE

HOMEWARD BOUND

For the return journey, Alexander planned to return to the Jhelum and then sail his army – together with all the women, children and pack animals that went with it – downriver until they came to the sea. (Not the Ocean at the End of the World that they'd been aiming for in the east, but the one at the southern edge of Asia.)

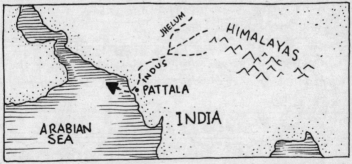

All together there were something like 120,000 people (and quite a bit of luggage), so on the banks of the Jhelum, Alex first had to put together a fleet of more than 1,000 ships. Some were commandeered from local tribes but many had to be built from scratch using timber felled from nearby forests. It was a tall order for an army that was already exhausted. (Imagine if you had to build your own plane when you wanted to come back from your holidays!)

Eventually, though, the new navy was ready to set sail.

Even with all those ships, there was only room for half of the soldiers in Alexander's army, and the others – with Hephaistion and Craterus in charge – marched down the riverbanks on foot.

At first Alexander relaxed on deck by listening to his court poets and historians read out stories from the books they'd written about his great exploits. But he soon got into a spot of difficulty when the fleet ran into a whirlpool and the Royal Flagship began to sink. Alex couldn't swim, of course, and had to be scrambled to safety by his friends. Still, it didn't stop him boasting that he'd now done battle with a great river, as well as with great armies!

And his battles with armies weren't over yet, because there were several powerful tribes that the Macedonians encountered on their journey south and they still had to do plenty of fighting. In one battle, Alex was struck through the chest with an arrow, and was seriously ill for weeks, confined to his tent. Rumours soon began to spread among the soldiers that he was dead, and he had his work cut out to stamp them out. In the end he was forced to haul himself on top of a horse and ride through the camp in front of his men, to show them he was still alive.

He was greeted with a storm of applause, which must have put a smile on his face in spite of the pain. Then he staggered back to his tent and passed out.

A few weeks later, by the time the river began to approach the sea, Alex was feeling much better, so he ordered his men to stop off at a place called Pattala and build an entire system of docks and harbours so that the fleet could put in for a refit. (That's a bit like having to build not just your own plane, but your own airport as well!) Then, leaving Hephaistion in charge of that little task, he went off with a smaller fleet to explore the coastal area further downstream.

GREAT STORIES

According to one story it was on this trip that Alex was caught out by something he'd never encountered before: low tide. The Mediterranean Sea around Greece has only very small tides, but the Indian Ocean has much larger ones. So Alex and his men were completely taken by surprise when they woke up one morning to find that the sea had disappeared!

Luckily, of course, it came back a few hours later and carried them back to Pattala.

Desert rats

Alexander's men didn't know it yet, but for many of them the worst part of the entire campaign was still to come. From Pattala, Alexander had decided to cover the next stage of the journey home by sending half of the army by sea, up the Persian Gulf, while the other half marched on land, along the barren coast of Gedrosia.

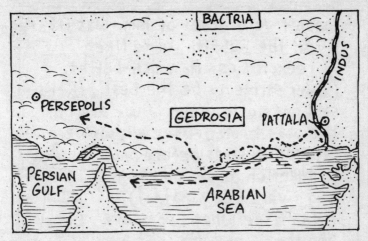

He couldn't send the whole army by sea, because with no ports along the coast to re-supply them, they'd run out of food and water before they got very far. So he would have to take half the army by land, stopping every so often not just to fight tribes, but to dig wells and collect food for the navy, as well as find good spots for the ships to put in and pick up the supplies. Unfortunately the Makran Desert, which they would have to cross, was one of the most unfriendly places anywhere on earth. But that didn't put Alexander off!

Alexander's Secret Diary
August 325 BC

I remember Aristotle telling me that the famous Persian king Cyrus the Great once tried to take his army across the Makran, and only seven of his men survived. Well, that

wasn't very great of him, was it?
Cyrus the Rubbish, more like.
I reckon I can do much better.
('Ever strive to be the best', that's
still my motto, even if we are on
the way home.) After all, we've
crossed deserts before (not
to mention mountain ranges
and rivers and whatnot).
I don't see what's so scary
about this one. It's just a
bit of sand, isn't it?

At first, all went fairly well. Alex's men were able to keep close to the shore, so there was no danger of getting lost, and the scariest thing they encountered was a stone-age tribe who lived in houses built of whalebones and had bad breath because of all the fish they ate.

However, the going soon got much rougher, and mountainous territory along the coast forced Alexander and his men further inland and into the worst part of the desert.

It wasn't long before they got lost in a sandstorm and became desperately short of drinking water and other supplies. (They certainly weren't able to provide any supplies for the fleet, which just had to manage without them.) After a few days, many of the party had been struck down by heatstroke from the burning sun, while wagons and pack animals sank in deep sand dunes that stretched to the horizon like waves of the sea.

Some men screamed in agony as their shoes filled with burning grit while others died painfully after being bitten by venomous snakes and prickled by poisonous plants. (According to one story, they even came across a sort of desert cucumber that squirted blinding juice into their eyes!)

Occasionally the men would come across a tiny well of brackish water, but they were so desperately thirsty that they couldn't hold back and many died as a result of drinking too much, too quickly.

Alexander's Secret Diary
October 325 BC

Well, I must admit, it's a tiny bit hard-going, but my men are dropping like flies. (Rather weedy of them, after all we've been through.) And as usual they're always bleating: 'Are we nearly there?' (To be honest, I don't know as I'm a bit lost.)

We came to one tiny well, but it had dried up and there was only enough water to fill a single helmet. Naturally, one of the men staggered over and presented me with it.

Well, I was feeling pretty parched, I must say, and I'd have liked to sink the lot. But then I remembered that a great leader must always make sacrifices. So I held out the helmet... and tipped the water on to the sand. (These grand gestures are necessary sometimes, to encourage the men!)

Pity about the poor chap who fetched it, though. He conked out after that. (Must have been overcome by my selfless act.)

In the end, after two whole months of trekking through the desert, Alexander did finally find his way back to the coast. But, although he didn't like to admit it, the trip had been a total disaster. On top of all the other calamities, thousands of the women and children travelling with the army had been swept away in a flash flood. Of the 85,000 people who'd set off with Alex, only a *quarter* survived.

STILL, I **TOLD** YOU I COULD DO BETTER THAN CYRUS THE SO-CALLED GREAT!

A WHOLE BUNCH OF WEDDINGS (AND TWO MORE FUNERALS)

Alexander wasn't in the best of moods after his little adventure in the Makran, and things didn't improve when he arrived at the agreed meeting place near Susa to find no sign of Nearchus or the fleet.

Alexander's Secret Diary
November 325 BC

Where on earth are they? I hope they haven't got lost - or worse still, drowned! That's not going to look good in the history books, is it? Not on top of the desert fiasco. (Not that I'm saying it __was__ a fiasco, but some people might see it that way.)

Maybe they've just gone on ahead? After all, we were in that desert for a teeny bit longer than

> planned. Maybe they gave us up for dead and went on without us. Mind you, that's not a very cheery thought either. Shows how much faith they've got in me.

Worse still, Alex soon started hearing bad things about what had been going on at the heart of his Persian Empire while he'd been exploring further east. It seemed that a number of the men that he'd appointed as satraps had been living it up and partying to excess, and to pay for it they'd been cheating him and stealing money from the royal coffers.

ALEXANDER WON'T BE BACK FOR YEARS. LET'S MAKE THE MOST OF IT.

Others had equipped themselves with private armies and set themselves up as independent rulers. One man, whom Alex had appointed as his Grand Imperial Treasurer in Babylon, had actually had the nerve to run off with an army of paid bandits and enough cash to last him a lifetime.

Alex was absolutely furious and soon set about putting his house in order. He dashed off letters to various satraps and senior officers, ordering them to disband their armies and summoning them to a place called Carmania. There he had most of them arrested and clapped in irons. Many of them were executed.

In their places he appointed new satraps, including a number of Persian noblemen. (By now Alexander had decided that they were sometimes more reliable than his own countrymen.)

Alex cheers up

Eventually, Nearchus turned up safe and sound, but he had only five companions with him and at first Alex assumed the navy had been lost. He must have been mighty relieved when he learnt that in fact the fleet was intact, and lay at anchor at a nearby port while undergoing repairs. Nearchus told Alex all about *their* adventures, including a story about how they'd been chased by a school of whales, but he and the other sailors had had a relatively easy time of it. In the end, they'd been able to gather their own supplies along the coast, and they'd suffered nothing like the ordeal of the miserable Makran march.

In customary Greek style, Alexander celebrated the safe return of the fleet with plenty of sacrifices to the gods and a fair bit of drinking too. He also put on a gigantic athletic contest and music competition...

AND GUESS WHO WON?

TWANG!

The ordeal in the desert had shaken Alexander, but now that he'd been reunited with his navy and asserted himself by executing a few rebellious satraps, he was feeling *much* better. So in a generous moment he rewarded his soldiers by cancelling all their debts (including any money they owed for all the wine they'd knocked back over the last few years!). He even sent home a load of Greek men who'd fought for the Persians as mercenaries – along with orders that they should be forgiven and treated well. Then he sorted out another little matter that had been on his mind lately…

The Macedonian Mail

Now available throughout Asia (except the really hilly bits) Summer 324 BC

ALEXANDER IS A GOD: IT'S OFFICIAL

After years of speculation, it has finally been confirmed: Alexander of Macedon is a god.

The official announcement came at the opening ceremony of this year's Olympic Games, in front of government leaders from all the Greek states. Alexander has decreed that from now on the official title 'god' is to be added to all his others

(including Pharaoh and Lord of All Asia).

Alexander himself, who is still on his campaigns, was unavailable for comment. However, his mother, Olympias, 47, said: 'I don't like to say "I told you so", but I always thought there was something special about that boy.'

Olympias: 'I told you so'

Some of the politicians who represented the city-states were furious at the announcement, whilst others treated it as a complete joke. Who on earth (or in heaven) did Alexander think he was?

Poor old Antipater, the man Alex had left in charge of Macedonia while he was away, was particularly offended. He'd had a hard time of it in recent years…

• Firstly, he'd had to deal with Greek states rebelling against him every five minutes, and then when he'd won a great battle against them he'd had to put up with Alex writing to tell him that compared to *his* great victories in Asia, that was nothing more than 'a battle among mice'.

• Secondly, he'd had to put up with Alex's interfering mum sticking her beak into his affairs, bossing him around and bad-mouthing him to Alex.

• And thirdly, he'd had to take it on the chin when he found out that Alexander had – on his mum's say-so – executed his own son-in-law (another Alexander) on suspicion of treachery.

So it was just adding insult to injury when he heard that Alexander now wanted to be officially known as a god. Antipater was a down-to-earth, old-fashioned sort who didn't stand for any newfangled nonsense, so he took a pretty dim view of *that* idea. It was one thing being a great conqueror – and no one could deny that Alex was that – but he was only human, after all. (And he'd made plenty of mistakes to prove it.)

Unfortunately, that wasn't how Alex saw it...

WELL, I MEAN, I AM RELATED TO HERACLES, AND *HE* ENDED UP TURNING INTO A GOD. AND DIDN'T ISOCRATES TELL DAD THAT IF HE CONQUERED ASIA THEN HE'D VIRTUALLY BE A GOD?

WELL, I *HAVE* CONQUERED ASIA, HAVEN'T I ? AND DON'T FORGET I'M A PHARAOH, AND THAT MAKES ME A SON OF RA. AND THEN THERE WAS THE ORACLE AT SIWAH WHO SAID...

One more sulk

Back on planet earth, Alex was soon in trouble with his men again, and found himself facing a second mutiny at a place called Opis (modern-day Baghdad). It all started when he told some of his Macedonian soldiers (about 10,000 of them) to go on home to Macedonia without him.

The soldiers had expected to return to Macedonia as conquering heroes, alongside their great leader. They'd been looking forward to it all the way back.

But they suddenly realized that without Alexander, they were likely to be treated not as heroes, but as retired soldiers who'd simply been thrown on the scrapheap.

They also realized that Macedonia was no longer the great place it had once been. In fact, Alexander hardly seemed interested in it at all anymore. Instead, he planned to make Babylon the capital of his empire, while Macedonia once more became little more than a backwater on the fringes of the action. Alexander had begun as a Macedonian setting out to conquer the Persian Empire, but the soldiers felt that in a way the Persian Empire had conquered *him*. After all, he'd appointed many Persians as satraps to govern his empire and he'd filled his army with thousands of Persian soldiers. The Macedonians were being sent home not as a well-earned reward for their years of service, but simply because Alexander no longer needed them.

Well they didn't like that idea one bit so they threw down their weapons and refused to budge.

In the end it took one of Alexander's great speeches (and a bit of a sulk in his tent) to bring his soldiers round to his point of view:

• First he reminded them that they had all benefited enormously from his father Philip's reign.

WITHOUT HIM, YOU'D BE NOTHING BUT SHEEP-FARMERS ON THE MOUNTAINS OF MACEDONIA.

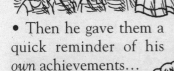

• Then he gave them a quick reminder of his *own* achievements…

AND A HUNDRED-AND-SEVENTY-FOURTHLY…

• Then he accused his men of being ungrateful, told them he'd have to rely only on *Persians* in future, and swept off to his tent in a huff.

Do not disturb, NOT EVER!

This did the trick, because the Macedonians were soon crying their eyes out and asking to be let in so they could tell Alex how grateful they were for all he'd done for them (even if they did have sore feet). Well, at the sight of all those tough old soldiers blubbing away, it wasn't long before Alexander himself burst into tears. And then they were all making up with a lot of manly bear-hugging (and probably a bit of kissing too).

In fact, Alex immediately ordered a great banquet to celebrate the fact that they were all friends again. The soldiers who had mutinied were given seats of honour alongside Alex and were even allowed to drink from the royal wine bowl. And although plenty of Persian soldiers were invited as well, they didn't get nearly such good seats.

The Macedonian soldiers just needed to be made to feel a bit special, really, and after the feast, Alex sent them home just as he'd planned. With them he sent Craterus, with orders to take over from Antipater, who was summoned to Babylon. However, Craterus got delayed on the way, and Antipater – who probably feared that Alex's mum had finally persuaded Alex to give him the chop – stayed at home and sent his son Cassander instead.

'I do, I do ... and so does everybody else!'

A little later, when Alex was in Susa, he went even further than he'd ever been before with his efforts to bring together the Macedonian and Persian factions in his court.

He ordered around 100 of the remaining Macedonian officers to marry girls from the very noblest Persian families. Everybody got married on the same day, and to set an example, even Alex got himself hitched (despite having one wife already) to *two* nice-looking Persian girls (including one of Darius' daughters).

Hephaistion also found himself married – to another of Darius' daughters – and everybody celebrated afterwards at a gigantic party that went on for five whole days!

Thinking about the future

Although he didn't want to go back to boring old Macedonia, Alexander didn't plan to settle down in Babylon either. There was certainly plenty to do there, since his new empire still needed a great deal of organizing, but Alex just wasn't one for sitting still and he had big ideas for further adventures.

> ## Things to do:
>
> • More exploring - eg Arabia, Africa and Europe
>
> • More conquering - eg Arabia, Africa and Europe
>
> • More striving - eg to be the best.

However, his plans were soon interrupted by unforeseen events...

One day Alexander was throwing one of his lavish parties to celebrate the annual festival of Dionysus, god of wine.

TWANG!

When suddenly Hephaistion collapsed on the ground and was rushed to bed with a fever.

His doctor put him on a strict diet for a week and he soon began to feel better.

So much so that he woke up early one morning and, behind the doctor's back, wolfed down a whole boiled chicken and half a gallon of chilled wine!

CHOMP!

Not surprisingly, Hephaistion soon began to feel unwell again, and this time there was no recovery…

The Macedonian Mail

Asian Edition - October 324 BC

HEPHAISTION DEAD:
AN EMPIRE MOURNS

Throughout the Empire, a period of official mourning begins today, following the death of the Great King's closest friend. Captain Hephaistion was a long-serving officer in the Macedonian armed forces, as well as a loyal adviser to King Alexander. He passed away this morning, apparently from 'complications' following a fever.

King Alexander is said to be devastated by the news, and sources close to the palace have confirmed that he threw himself on top of Hephaistion's body and lay there for hours, sobbing like a baby.

Funeral-pyre plans: more inside

As a mark of respect he has cut his hair, trimmed the manes of his horses, and banned all musical instruments from court until further notice.

Hephaistion's body is to be embalmed and sent to Babylon for the grandest state funeral ever seen.

King Alexander has ordered every province of the Empire to contribute to the expenses.

• Hephaistion's doctor executed for being useless. Full story, page 2.
• 'I snogged Hephy once'. Ex-lover tells all, page 3.

The death of Hephaistion was a real blow, and Alexander was never really the same again. He carried on preparing for further conquests, of course, but he became increasingly depressed and spent more and more time day-dreaming or drinking himself stupid. He also seemed to see bad omens everywhere he looked…

Spring 323 BC

Dear Mum,
The other day we were sailing down the River Euphrates, inspecting it to see if it would be OK to carry my new Arabian fleet. Suddenly there was a gust of wind and my royal sun hat blew right off.
I wasn't that bothered, and was just knotting a hankie to use instead, but then someone pointed out that my hat had got caught in some reeds that were right next to an ancient

> royal tomb of some Assyrian Kings. Well, I just sat there thinking that obviously it can only mean one thing ...I'm next. I'm going to die - just like Hephaistion - and be buried like those ancient Kings!!! Your worried son, Alex x x x

Back in Babylon, it wasn't long before Alexander's fears were realized…

One evening, after a banquet in honour of Nearchus, Alexander was feeling a bit low and was just on his way to bed when he was persuaded to join some friends who were off to a late-night party. No doubt they told him that the best way to shake off the blues was to go out and enjoy himself, and Alex was soon doing just that.

Alex was rushed back to his quarters and put to bed, but he awoke the next day with a dreadful hangover and a high fever. It didn't stop him wining and dining again the following night, but then his fever grew much, much worse. From his bed, he carried on giving daily briefings to his officers, but it soon became clear that his days were numbered.

As rumours of his poor health spread, Macedonian troops surrounded his palace, clambering to be let in to see their Great King and pay their last respects. (There were so many of them that a special hole had to be knocked in the wall.)

And among his senior officers there was one desperately important question that they all wanted to ask: had he chosen a successor?

GREAT TIMES: THE SUCCESSION

Alexander's mentally ill half-brother Arrhidaeus was technically next in line for the throne. But everyone knew Arrhidaeus wasn't capable of ruling an empire by himself. Luckily, Alex's Persian wife, Roxane, was now pregnant with his child, but no one yet knew if the baby would be a boy or a girl. And of course, even it were a boy, it would be years before he'd be grown up enough to govern. So everybody knew that in practice it would be one of Alexander's top generals who would rule the Empire. The question was, which one?

WELL, LET ME THINK... I KNOW! I GIVE MY EMPIRE TO... THE **GREATEST** AMONG YOU!

Alex always liked a competition, and by refusing to name a successor he made sure that his officers would fight each other tooth and nail for his crown. It certainly wasn't the best way to preserve his empire intact, but it was Alexander all over.

Alexander the Great died on 10 June, 323 BC. His last words were reported to be…

I FORESEE A GREAT CONTEST AT MY FUNERAL.

GREAT STORIES: WAS ALEX MURDERED?

Not everyone thinks it was the binge-drinking that killed Alexander. Many people think he may have caught malaria or some other disease, while some even argue that he was deliberately poisoned. There was certainly no shortage of people who might have wanted to bump him off. Among the chief suspects are:

Antipater – fed up with being bullied by Alexander and his mum, and beginning to fear for his position and his life. Also cross about Alex claiming to be a god.

Cassander – Antipater's son, an ambitious young man who fancied his chances as king. (Once had his head banged against a wall by Alex after laughing at someone for bowing down before him.)

Craterus and Perdiccas – ambitious Macedonian officers who hoped to inherit his throne.

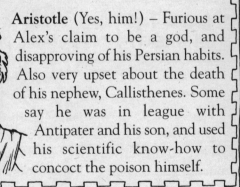

Aristotle (Yes, him!) – Furious at Alex's claim to be a god, and disapproving of his Persian habits. Also very upset about the death of his nephew, Callisthenes. Some say he was in league with Antipater and his son, and used his scientific know-how to concoct the poison himself.

171

AFTER ALEX

Alexander's body was embalmed in spices to keep it from rotting and then sent in a magnificent funeral procession to Egypt, where he was buried. (Unfortunately, though, the exact location of the tomb has since been lost.)

LOST? OH, GREAT!

By the time of his death, aged 32, Alexander had travelled to the furthest reaches of the known world and conquered an empire of almost unimaginable size. He'd led his army across mountains, deserts, rivers and seas, and he'd won victory after victory against impossible odds. And all in little more than ten years. It's easy to see why he soon picked up the nickname by which he's still known today: '*Mega-Alexandros*' – which is Greek for 'Alexander the Great'.

However, Alex wasn't nearly as good at looking after his empire as he was at winning it, and in the end it didn't last very long – mainly as a result of bickering between the various people who thought they should inherit it. Here's what happened…

• Roxane's baby did turn out to be a boy, named Alexander after his father. At first, he and his uncle – Alex's half-brother Arrhidaeus – ruled the Empire between them.

• However, the real power lay with Antipater, who ran the empire on their behalf, until his death in 319 BC.

• Antipater's son Cassander then took over, and – on the advice of Alex's mum Olympias – murdered both Arrhidaeus and his wife.

• Eventually, Cassander got fed up with Olympias, and ordered *her* execution as well. (Which probably served her right, all things considered.)

• Then, just for good measure, little Alexander (our Alex's son, now 13) was *also* murdered by Cassander, along with *his* mother Roxane.

That left Cassander and several other officers who'd once served loyally under Alexander to fight it out bitterly in the 'Wars of the Successors'.

By the time the dust had settled, Alexander's Empire had been torn apart, with each man proclaiming himself king of the various bits he'd managed to grab:

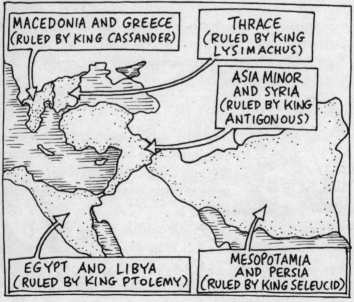

MACEDONIA AND GREECE (RULED BY KING CASSANDER)

THRACE (RULED BY KING LYSIMACHUS)

ASIA MINOR AND SYRIA (RULED BY KING ANTIGONOUS)

EGYPT AND LIBYA (RULED BY KING PTOLEMY)

MESOPOTAMIA AND PERSIA (RULED BY KING SELEUCID)

For years after Alex's death, Macedonia stayed in charge in Greece, despite further rebellions from the city-states. And thanks to the various Greek kings who ruled there, as well as all those Greek cities Alex had founded, Greek language and Greek ideas spread throughout much of Asia and the Middle East for centuries to come. But almost nothing remained of Alexander's conquests in India, except legendary tales of a superman called 'Sikander'. And the idea of a single worldwide empire was over, at least until the Romans came along a couple of hundred years later.

The Romans were great admirers of Alex's exploits and many of their emperors tried to copy him. But Alex wasn't admired by *everyone*, and in Persia itself he soon became known as 'Iskander the Accursed'. To some people he has always been a noble conqueror who brought two civilizations closer together, while to others he was a bloodthirsty monster who brought little more than pain and suffering to the people he met. But love him or loathe him, just about *everyone* agrees that his is one of the most famous names in history.

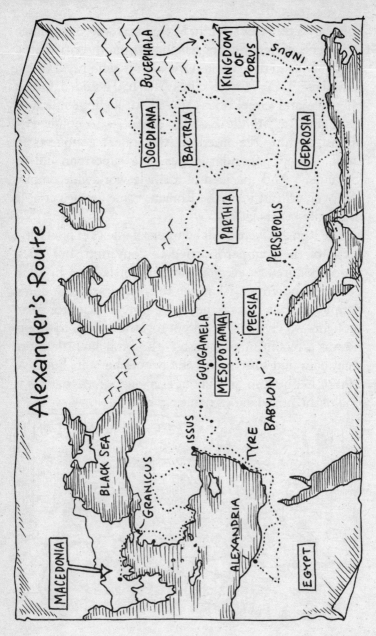